Fourth Workshop on South and Southeast Asian Natural Language Processing

(WSSANLP 2013)

Held at the 6th International Joint Conference on Natural Language Processing (IJCNLP 2013)

Nagoya, Japan
14 – 18 October 2013

ISBN: 978-1-62993-547-8

Printed from e-media with permission by:

Curran Associates, Inc.
57 Morehouse Lane
Red Hook, NY 12571

proceedings.com

Some format issues inherent in the e-media version may also appear in this print version.

Printed by Curran Associates, Inc. (2014)

Association for Computational Linguistics
209 N. Eighth Street
Stroudsburg, Pennsylvania 18360

Phone: 1-570-476-8006
Fax: 1-570-476-0860

acl@aclweb.org

Additional copies of this publication are available from:

Curran Associates, Inc.
57 Morehouse Lane
Red Hook, NY 12571 USA
Phone: 845-758-0400
Fax: 845-758-2634
Email: curran@proceedings.com
Web: www.proceedings.com

We wish to thank our sponsors and supporters!

Platinum Sponsors

NLP

www.anlp.jp

Silver Sponsors

Google™

www.google.com

Bronze Sponsors

Rakuten

www.rakuten.com

Supporters

NAGOYA CONVENTION
& VISITORS BUREAU

Nagoya Convention & Visitors Bureau

We wish to thank our organizers!

Organizers

Asian Federation of Natural Language Processing (AFNLP)

Toyohashi University of Technology

This page intentionally left blank.

Preface

Welcome to the 4th Workshop on South and Southeast Asian Natural Language Processing (WSSANLP - 2013), a collocated event at the 6th International Joint Conference on Natural Language Processing (IJCNLP 2013) , 14 - 18 October, 2013. South Asia comprises of the countries, Afghanistan, Bangladesh, Bhutan, India, Maldives, Nepal, Pakistan and Sri Lanka. Southeast Asia, on the other hand, consists of Brunei, Burma, Cambodia, East Timor, Indonesia, Laos, Malaysia, Philippines, Singapore, Thailand and Vietnam.

This area is the home to thousands of languages that belong to different language families like Indo-Aryan, Indo-Iranian, Dravidian, Sino-Tibetan, Austro-Asiatic, Kradai, Hmong-Mien, etc. In terms of population, South Asian and Southeast Asia represent 35 percent of the total population of the world which means as much as 2.5 billion speakers. Some of the languages of these regions have a large number of native speakers: Hindi (5th largest according to number of its native speakers), Bengali (6th), Punjabi (12th), Tamil(18th), Urdu (20th), etc.

As internet and electronic devices including PCs and hand held devices including mobile phones have spread far and wide in the region, it has become imperative to develop language technology for these languages. It is important for economic development as well as for social and individual progress.

A characteristic of these languages is that they are under-resourced. The words of these languages show rich variations in morphology. Moreover they are often heavily agglutinated and synthetic, making segmentation an important issue. The intellectual motivation for this workshop comes from the need to explore ways of harnessing the morphology of these languages for higher level processing. The task of morphology, however, in South and Southeast Asian Languages is intimately linked with segmentation for these languages.

The goal of WSSANLP is:

• Providing a platform to linguistic and NLP communities for sharing and discussing ideas and work on South and Southeast Asian languages and combining efforts.
• Development of useful and high quality computational resources for under resourced South and Southeast Asian languages.

We are delighted to present to you this volume of proceedings of the 4th Workshop on South and Southeast Asian Natural Language Processing. We have received total 15 submission in the categories of long paper and short paper. On the basis of our review process, we have competitively selected 9 long (regular) papers for oral presentations and 3 short papers for poster presentations.

We look forward to an invigorating workshop.

Pushpak Bhattacharyya (Chair WSSANLP-2013),
Indian Institute of Technology Bombay, India

M.G. Abbas Malik (Chair of Organizing Committee WSSANLP-2013),
Faculty of Computing and Information Technology (North Jeddah Branch),
King Abdulaziz University, Saudi Arabia

The Fourth Workshop on South and Southeast Asian Natural Language processing WSSANLP-2013

Workshop Chair:

Pushpak Bhattacharyya, Indian Institute of Technoloyg Bombay, India

Workshop Organization Co-chair:

M. G. Abbas Malik, King Abdulaziz University, Saudi Arabia

Invited Speaker:

Dekai Wu, HKUST Human Language Technology Center

Organizers:

Aasim Ali, Punjab University College of Information Technology, University of the Punjab, Pakistan
Amitava Das, Jadavpur Univeristy, India

Program Committee:

Sadaf Abdul Rauf, Fatima Jinnah Women University, Pakistan
Naveed Afzal, King Abdulaziz University, Saudi Arabia
Aasim Ali, University of the Punjab, Pakistan
M. Waqas Anwar, COMSATS Institute of Information Technology, Pakistan
Bal Krishna Bal, Kathmandu University, Nepal
Sivaji Bandyopadhyay, Jadavpur University, India
Laurent Besacier, GETALP-LIG, Université de Grenoble, France
Pushpak Bhattacharyya, IIT Bombay, India
Hervé Blanchon, GETALP-LIG, Université de Grenoble, France
Christian Boitet, GETALP-LIG, Université de Grenoble, France
Amitava Das, Norwegian University of Science and Technology, Norway
Alain Desoulieres, INALCO Paris, France
Choochart Haruechaiyasak, NECTEC, Thailand
Sarmad Hussain, Al-Khawarizmi Institute of Computer Science, University of Engineering and Technology, Pakistan
Aravind K. Joshi, University of Pennsylvania, USA
Abid Khan, University of Peshawar, Pakistan
Imtiaz Hussain Khan, King Abdulaziz University, Saudi Arabia
A. Kumaran, Microsoft Research, India
Haizhou Li, Institute for Infocomm Research, Singapore
M. G. Abbas Malik, King Abdulaziz University - North Jeddah Branch, Saudi Arabia

Table of Contents

Workshop Program

Friday October 18, 2013

(9:30 - 9:40) Openning Session

(9:40 - 10:35) Invited Talk

\+ by Prof. Dekai Wu, HKUST Human Language Technology Center

(10:35 - 10:50) Coffee Break

Session Regular Papers 1: (10:50 - 12:30) WSSANLP Session 1

10:50 *Fast Bootstrapping of Grapheme to Phoneme System for Under-resourced Languages - Application to the Iban Language*
Sarah Samson Juan and Laurent Besacier

11:15 *LexToPlus: A Thai Lexeme Tokenization and Normalization Tool*
Choochart Haruechaiyasak and Alisa Kongthon

11:40 *A Three-Layer Architecture for Automatic Post Editing System Using Rule-Based Paradigm*
Mahsa Mohaghegh, Abdolhossein Sarrafzadeh and Mehdi Mohammadi

12:05 *Statistical Stemming for Kannada*
Suma Bhat

(12:30 - 13:30) Lunch break

Friday October 18, 2013 (continued)

Session Regular Papers 2: (13:30 - 14:45) WSSANLP Session 2

13:30 *On Application of Conditional Random Field in Stemming of Bengali Natural Language Text*
Sandipan Sarkar and Sivaji Bandyopadhyay

13:55 *Urdu Hindi Machine Transliteration using SMT*
M. G. Abbas Malik, Christian Boitet, Laurent Besacier and Pushpak Bhattcharyya

14:20 *Urdu Spell Checking: Reverse Edit Distance Approach*
Saadat Iqbal, Muhammad Waqas Anwar, Usama Ijaz Bajwa and Zobia Rehman

(14:45 - 15:00) Coffee Break

Session Poster Papers: (15:00 - 15:50) WSSANLP Session 3

15:00 *Information Mining from Islamic Scriptures*
Abdul Rauf Saeed and Syed Waqar Jaffry

15:25 *English to Urdu Hierarchical Phrase-based Statistical Machine Translation*
Nadeem Khan, Muhammad Waqas Anwar, Usama Ijaz Bajwa and Nadir Durrani

Session Regular Papers 3: (15:50 - 16:40) WSSANLP Session 4

15:50 *Cliticization and Endoclitics Generation of Pashto Language*
Azizud Din

16:15 *Malayalam Clause Boundary Identifier: Annotation and Evaluation*
Sobha Lalitha Devi and Lakshmi S

Friday October 18, 2013 (continued)

(16:40 - 17:00) Closing Remarks

Fast Bootstrapping of Grapheme to Phoneme System for Under-resourced Languages - Application to the Iban Language

Sarah Samson Juan, Laurent Besacier
Laboratoire d'Informatique de Grenoble / Grenoble University
Grenoble, France
sarah.samson-juan@imag.fr, laurent.besacier@imag.fr

Abstract

This paper deals with the fast bootstrapping of Grapheme-to-Phoneme (G2P) conversion system, which is a key module for both automatic speech recognition (ASR), and text-to-speech synthesis (TTS). The idea is to exploit language contact between a local dominant language (Malay) and a very under-resourced language (Iban - spoken in Sarawak and in several parts of the Borneo Island) for which no resource nor knowledge is really available. More precisely, a pre-existing Malay G2P is used to produce phoneme sequences of Iban words. The phonemes are then manually post-edited (corrected) by an Iban native. This resource, which has been produced in a semi-supervised fashion, is later used to train the first G2P system for Iban language. As a by-product of this methodology, the analysis of the "pronunciation distance" between Malay and Iban enlighten the phonological and orthographic relations between these two languages. The experiments conducted show that a rather efficient Iban G2P system can be obtained after only two hours of post-edition (correction) of the output of Malay G2P applied to Iban words.

1 Introduction

Multilingualism is at the heart of current issues relating to cultural, economic and social exchanges in a globalized world. Thus, people are more likely to evolve in multilingual environments, as evidenced by recent trends of world and society: increasing importance of international organizations (multilateral organizations like European Union, multinational corporations, etc.), increase of cultural exchanges and travel, extensive use of social networks to communicate with people around the world, renewed interest in regional languages and dialects which now coexist with the national languages. Such "language diversity" must be taken into account. Moreover, it is known that among the most widely spoken languages in the world, many are those for which the technologies for written and spoken natural language processing are poorly developed (under-resourced languages). There is a commercial interest in enabling the ~300 most widely spoken languages in the digital domain: if digital technologies work for this group of languages that represents 95 % of humanity. As mobile phones are nearly ubiquitous (87 % penetration worldwide) and global internet access is approaching 1/3 of the human population, enabling "the long tail of languages" in the digital domain increasingly matters. The other ~6,500 languages are not of commercial interest, but there are other reasons to enable them if possible: to provide access to information, to provide a critical new domain of use for endangered languages, for better linguistic knowledge of them, for response in a crisis (surge languages), etc.

In this paper, our work concentrates on Grapheme-to-Phoneme (G2P) conversion system, which is an important component for both automatic speech recognition (ASR) and text-to-speech synthesis (TTS). We proposed a quick and plausible solution in developing a G2P system for an under-resourced language using existing G2P system with a language of the same family. More precisely, a pre-existing G2P of a local dominant language, Malay, is utilized to generate phoneme sequences for Iban, a language from the same family. The outputs are further post-edited manually by an Iban native to get the right sequences. The post-edited transcript is later used to train the first Iban G2P system. An alternative approach is also studied where we experiment on Phoneme-to-Phoneme (P2P) system which translates from

Malay pronunciation (output of a Malay G2P) to Iban pronunciation.

This paper is organized as follows: section 2 describes the languages involved in our work and their relationship is detailed in section 3. Section 4 presents our methodology for fast bootstrapping of Iban G2P system with the help of pre-existing Malay G2P and details of the P2P as well as our experimental results of this study. Last but not least, section 5 concludes this work and provides some perspectives.

2 Malay and Iban Languages

Malay and Iban languages are both spoken in Malaysia. The latter is mostly spoken only by the Iban community while Malay language has many speakers as it is the country's national language. In the following section, we briefly describe about the two languages and the resources that are currently available for our research.

2.1 Malay language and its G2P system

Globally, Malay is not only spoken in Malaysia but also in several other neighboring countries such as Brunei, Indonesia, Singapore and southern Thailand. Although it is spoken across several countries, each country has its own standard of pronunciation and spelling. For our study, we only focus on the Malay language spoken in Malaysia. This language is written using Latin alphabet and considered as an agglutinative language. An agglunative language has words that are formed by adding affixes onto a root word, word composition or reduplication (Rainavo-Malançon, 2004). Furthermore, it is not a tonal language like Mandarin or Vietnamese languages and basically, language users can distinguish general pronunciations directly from the grapheme sequences.

The Malay data that we applied in this study was collected by Universiti Sains Malaysia in Malaysia, which was used to design a Malay speech recognition system. Tan et al. (2009) collected Malay texts from 1998-2008 articles concerning economy, entertainment, sports and general news. The authors built a pronunciation dictionary and language model for the Malay ASR using these texts. From our observation, a total of 76.05K pronunciations was available for 63.9K distinct Malay words (36 different phonemes are used to transcribe Malay words).

To build our Malay G2P system, we utilized a data driven G2P toolkit called Phonetisaurus (Novak, 2012) using the Malay data as our training set. The open source toolkit is able to perform Expectation Maximization (EM)-based alignments between grapheme and phoneme sequences; it also uses a "target" N-gram language model (made up of phone sequences). Models are converted to weighted finite states tranducers (WFST) by Phonetisaurus for decoding.

Our Malay G2P model was constructed from 68K Malay pronunciations taken from the 76K total set (8.05K remain for testing). In our case, the target N-gram model uses $N = 7$ where the model was generated using original Kneser-Ney smoothing utilizing the SRILM toolkit (Stolcke, 2002). This model was chosen among several N-gram models where N values ranged from 3 to 7 and the 7-gram model gave us the lowest phoneme and word error rates compared to the rest.

We tested with the remaining 8.05K data to measure the accuracy of the Malay G2P system and the results are 6.20% phoneme error rate (PER) and 24.98% word error rate (WER). From this point, this system became the starting point before the development of the second language phonetizer, the Iban G2P system. First, we briefly explain about the target language and the preliminary text data available in the next part of this paper.

2.2 Iban language and its initial text resource

2.2.1 Brief background

The Iban language is mainly spoken among the Iban community, one of Sarawak's indigenous group in Malaysia. Sarawak is the biggest state in Malaysia and has more than 690,000 Ibans living across the region (Statistics-Department, 2010). Like Malay, the Iban language belongs to the Malayo-Polynesian branch of the Austronesian language family and Iban falls in the Ibanic language group (Lewis et al., 2013). Speakers can also be found in several parts of the Borneo Island such as in Kalimantan, Indonesia; however, we limit our focus to Iban system from Sarawak. Since the early 90s, schools in the region teaches Iban in the primary and secondary level as a nonobligatory subject. The teaching effort has also recently spread to the university level, where several universities open basic Iban courses for undergraduate students. Despite the fact there are many Iban speakers, resources for human language technologies (HLTs) are still very limited. Thus, we view this language as a very under-resourced language for technology applications.

2.2.2 Text resources

We began an Iban text collection campaign in November 2012: a total of 7000 articles was extracted from a local newspaper through its website. Articles dated from 2009 (the year when Iban articles started to be published online) to 2012, were mostly on general news, entertainment and sports. These articles were compiled and normalized. The steps in the text normalization process included removing HTML tags, changing numbers to words, converting commonly used abbreviations such as Apr. for April, Dr. for *Doktor* , Kpt. for *Kapten* and Prof. for *Profesor*, spliting paragraphs to sentences and removing punctuation marks except for '-'. For the latter step, we treated words "tied" with '-' as a single item. In Iban as well as in Malay, these words are categorized as reduplication or *jaku pengawa betandu penuh* in Iban. It is common that words are duplicated to form plurals and new words. Plurals are, for example, *bup-bup* or *rumah-rumah* or new words, such as, *bebai-bai*, *diuji-uji*, *ngijap-ngijapka* and *beberap-berap* where these words are categorized as partial reduplication. The final normalization step was to convert all capital words to lower case. After the text normalization process completed, we obtained approximately 2.08 M words. Based on this newly acquired corpus and the Malay corpus, we carried out a study on the relationship between Iban and Malay languages.

3 Malay-Iban relationship

3.1 Phonology

According to a reference manual written by the Centre of Curriculum and Sarawak Education Department (Education-Department, 2007), the Iban system is said to be influenced by the Malay system in terms of phonology, morphology and syntax. Omar (1981) provided the first description of the language in 1981 where among her work included the classifications of phonemes for Iban. There are 19 consonants (including semivowels), 6 vowels and 11 vowel clusters. Meanwhile for Malay, Tan et al. (2009) referred to Maris (1979)'s classification of Malay sounds. Based on Maris' work, there are 27 consonants, 6 vowels and 3 diphthongs. From the descriptions made by Omar and Maris, we carried out a comparative study between Malay and Iban phonemes.

Iban vs. Malay	Phonemes
Common	Consonants: p, b, m, w,t,d,n,ʧ,dʒ, s,l,r, ɲ, j, k, g, ŋ,h,ʔ Vowels : a,e,ə,i,o,u V. Clusters: ai, au
Difference	(only appear in Malay) Consonants: f,v,θ, z, x, ɣ, ð, ʃ (only appear in Iban) V. Clusters : ui,ia, ea,ua,oa,iu,iə, uə,oə

Table 1: *Iban and Malay common and different phonemes*

In Table 1, we present the common and different Malay and Iban consonants, vowels and vowel clusters. It is observed that Iban is a subset of Malay consonants and vowels. However, the same could not be said for Iban vowel clusters. These vowel clusters appear as variations in Iban pronunciations and we found that only two of the Iban vowel clusters, /ai/ and /au/ matched with Malay diphthongs, /aj/ and /aw/, respectively. Our next example of Iban words (refer to Table 2) also show that the missing vowel clusters are not expressed in the spellings (grapheme sequences). Hence, it is clear that a Malay G2P will produce incorrect phoneme sequences for Iban words due to the missing phonemes.

Vowel clusters	Phoneme and grapheme sequences
/ai/	/kumbai/ $\sim$ kumbai
/ui/	/ukui/ $\sim$ ukui
/ia/	/kiaʔ/ $\sim$ kiak
/ea/	/rumeah/ $\sim$ rumah
/ua/	/kuap/ $\sim$ kuap
/oa/	/menoa/ $\sim$ menua
/iu/	/niup/ $\sim$ niup
/au/	/tawn/ $\sim$ taun
/iə/	/biliəʔ/ $\sim$ bilik
/uə/	/puən/ $\sim$ pun
/oə/	/boəʔ/ $\sim$ buk

Table 2: *Iban vowel clusters with the related grapheme and phoneme sequences*

3.2 Orthography

Orthography relates to the standard writing system for a particular language. Both Malay and Iban are written using latin alphabets and their orthography system is closely related. Ng et al. (2009) investigated their orthographic similarity i.e; finding cognates and non-cognates between Malay and Iban. They applied several methods such as the Levenshtein distance (Levenshtein, 1966) in order to estimate the distances on 200 word pairs. Chosen words were translations of a Swadesh list (Swadesh, 1952), which is a common reference created for linguists to study relationships between languages. Ng et al. (2009) discovered that Iban has the highest cognate percentage of 61% with Malay compared to other Sarawak languages like Kelabit, Melanau and Bidayuh. From this observation, we investigated, at a larger scale, the pronunciation similarity between Iban and Malay words that have the same surface form.

There are 36,358 distinctive words in our Iban texts. From this lexicon, we identified words (surface forms) that match in both Malay and Iban lexicons. Table 3 shows that more than thirteen thousand words are shared between Malay, Iban and also surprisingly English. After removing words included in the CMU English pronunciation dictionary, the number of Malay-Iban common surface forms is 8,472 words.

Corpus	Vocab. size	Identical words	
		with English	w/o English
Malay	76,050	13,774	8,472
Iban	36,358		

Table 3: *Number of identical (same surface form) words found in our Iban and Malay lexicons*

Conclusively, 23% (8,472) of our Iban vocabulary is shared with Malay, 19% (6,707) with English, while the remaining 58% (21,179) purely belong to the Iban language. In other words, 42% of this lexicon is found shared not only with one, but, with two languages, English and Malay. This gave us an idea of language contact and code switching issues related to Iban language.

3.3 Measuring Malay-Iban pronunciation distance

To measure pronunciation distances, our concern was on Malay-Iban common surface forms only. The purpose was to study what was the minimum cost to transform a Malay phoneme sequences to an Iban one. We chose Levenshtein distance as the estimation method following the study by Heeringa and de Wet (2008). To carry out this investigation, we selected 100 most frequent common surface forms and prepared the pronunciation transcripts. Malay G2P was employed to generate an initial pronunciation transcript for Iban and the transcript was later post-edited by a native speaker.

The Levenshtein distance was computed for all 100 pronunciation pairs. As a result, we obtained 17% of errors (phoneme Insertions, Substitutions, Deletions) between Malay and Iban pronunciations but we found out that 47% of the Malay pronunciations were kept unchanged for Iban! This result confirms that the use of a Malay G2P is probably a good starting point to bootstrap an Iban G2P system. To put this result in perspective, we quote the work of Heeringa and de Wet (2008) who measured the average distance between Afrikaans and Dutch pronunciations and found that it was significantly smaller than between Afrikaans and Frisian ; as well as between Afrikaans and German.

No.	Words	Iban	Malay
1	ke	/kə/	/kə/
2	nya	/ɲaʔ/	/ɲə/ or / ɲa/
3	iya	/ija/	/ija/
4	ba	/baʔ/	/ba/
5	dua	/duwa/	/duwə/ or /duwa/
6	sida	/sidaʔ/	/sida/
7	puluh	/puluəh/	/puloh/
8	raban	/raban/	/raban/
9	lalu	/lalu/	/lalu/
10	orang	/urang/	/orang/

Table 4: *Example of ten words with phoneme sequences for Iban and Malay*

Table 4 shows an example of words and their corresponding Malay / Iban phoneme sequences. We analyzed several phonemes that were frequently substituted and inserted in the Malay-to-Iban transformation process. The phoneme /o/ is frequently substituted with /uə/ , for example, the word *puluh* in Table 4 is transcribed as /puloh/ in Malay while in Iban, it is /puluəh/. This substitution occurred due to the vowel cluster /uə/ in Iban utterance. Also, we found out that phoneme /e/ was frequently substituted by /iə/ in sequences such as /pəsiser/ in Malay to /pəsisiər/ in Iban for the word *pesisir*. The glottal stop /ʔ/ was inserted at almost all words ending with a vowel. As an example, *kepala* transcribed as /kəpala/ in Malay needs a glottal stop at the final vowel to transform to /kəpalaʔ/ and another example, *nya*, changes from /ɲa/ to /ɲaʔ/.

To summarize, this preliminary study on Malay-Iban pronunciation distance suggested that the Malay G2P system can be used as a basis for transcribing Iban words. The suggestion was also supported by the closeness of these two languages based on phonological and orthographical aspects particularly for Malay-Iban cognates. However, we need to investigate the Malay G2P performance on non-related / non-common words specifically, the "pure" Iban words in the lexicon. The strategy is detailed and experimented in the following section.

4 Obtaining Iban G2P training data via post-editing the Malay G2P output

4.1 Methodology

Our proposed methodology involves the following process:

- Choose two different development sets of common Malay-Iban and pure Iban words, from the Iban vocabulary.
- Apply Malay G2P model on each set to obtain initial phoneme sequences.
- Post edit Malay G2P outputs to produce correct Iban pronunciations and measure time taken to complete this phase.
- Train Iban pronunciations from previous step as a first Iban G2P system (using Phonetisaurus)
- Run and evaluate both Malay and Iban G2P systems on new Iban test set

We chose two sets of 500 most frequent Iban words (500 common Malay-Iban and 500 pure Iban words) and then applied our Malay G2P system to convert words into phoneme sequences. Then, a native speaker manually edited the output to obtain correct sequences for Iban. Moreover, we identified phonemes that were frequently substituted or inserted during the process and measured the phoneme and word (sequence) error rates using a scoring toolkit by the National Institute of Standards and Technology (NIST, 2010). Thereafter, we combined the post-edited transcripts into one list and trained our first Iban G2P system.

Upon achieving this, we selected another two sets of different words from the Iban vocabulary to evaluate the Malay G2P again and the new Iban G2P system. The two sets contain second 500 most frequent Iban words (500 common Malay-Iban and 500 pure Iban words).

4.2 G2P output evaluation

Phonetizer	Corpus	PER (%)	WER (%)	Post-edit (mins)
Malay G2P	500_{IM}	6.52	27.2	30
	500_{I}	15.8	56.0	42
Iban G2P	500_{IM}	13.6	44.2	45
	500_{I}	8.2	31.8	32
Iban P2P	500_{IM}	16.6	53.5	-
	500_{I}	7.3	31.9	-

Note: IM for common Malay-Iban words and I for pure Iban words

Table 5: *Malay G2P and Iban G2P systems (+ Iban P2P) peformance for an Iban phonetisation task*

Our first 1000 sequences generated by the Malay G2P scored at 11.88% PER and 48.9% WER. The scoring was based on the post-edited transcript that was completed by the native within 1 hour and 34 minutes. Now, Table 5 presents the evaluation results of our Iban G2P output and of Malay G2P, for comparison which was done on a second 1000 words data set. The test sets, 500_{IM} and 500_{I}, were taken from the second most frequent items in the Iban lexicon. The values presented are phoneme error rate (PER), word error rate (WER) and post-editing effort in minutes. Based on these results, we discovered that the Malay G2P system performed best for Malay-Iban matching words and the result is consistent with Malay G2P performance on Malay test set. On the other hand, the Iban G2P system gave better results for pure Iban words. Despite of the small amount of data used to train the Iban G2P (1000 sentences), it was able to perform less than 10% PER. The time spent to correct Iban G2P output was also less for pure Iban words compared to the post-editing effort for Malay G2P output. However, the Iban G2P system seems to be not suitable to phonetize common Malay-Iban words (PER increases from 6.52 % to 13.6 %).

We examined in detail on each G2P outputs to find wrongly substituted and deleted phonemes. In the case of pure Iban words test results, Malay G2P substituted phonemes /uə/, /iə/, /ea/, with /o/, /e/ and /a/, respectively, while the glottal stop /ʔ/ and phoneme /r/ were missed out. Meanwhile, Iban G2P substituted phonemes /ə/ for /e/, /iə/ for /i/, /uə/ for /u/ and /uə/ for /o/. We also found that the glottal stop was inaccurately inserted. As for the Malay-Iban common words results, similar phonemes were wrongly predicted by both G2P systems. However, Malay G2P conversion was more accurate compared to Iban G2P because many original phoneme sequences were retained for Iban due to Malay word adoption (e.g; words such as *parlimen* (parliament), *menteri* (minister) and *muzik* (music)). For pure Iban words, Iban G2P gave better sequences because it included vowel clusters (combined Malay phonemes) that were missing in the initial Malay G2P.

4.3 Converting pure Iban words using P2P system

Apart from the phonetization tasks by G2P models, we also developed P2P system and conducted phonetization tasks using P2P phonetizer. Recalling our Malay G2P outputs which was later post-edited to get data for Iban G2P system, we took these outputs and the corrected pronunciations as the training corpus for an Iban P2P system.

For experimentation, the 1000 pairs of phoneme sequences were randomized and then divided into 10 portions. Later, we built ten systems with different training data sizes (add one portion to training set after each model developed) and evaluated the systems on pure Iban words.

All phone error rates acquired from applying the G2P and P2P systems were plotted as shown in Figure 1 (see non-dotted line). The results are between 6.4% to 7.6% and found to be rather stable for the P2P model. Also on the same graph, we plotted PERs that were obtained by applying 10 Iban G2P systems of different training data sizes where each system had the same Iban phoneme sequences as in each P2P system. Based on our results, the G2P systems gave worse results compared to the P2P systems' results. Unlike the slightly unstable P2P results, phone accuracy improved gradually after adding more data in the G2P. Finally, using 1000 words for training, Iban P2P and G2P systems' PER results are quite close and both systems have equal WER (31.9% - see also last line of table 5).

4.4 Phonetization of our whole Iban lexicon and final evaluation

Given results obtained, we decided to build the pronunciation lexicon for Iban using both G2P modules (Malay and Iban). The strategy was as follows: the Malay G2P phonetizes all Malay-Iban common words while the Iban G2P phonetizes all pure Iban words. In total, we phonetized 29,651 words (Iban-English not included) automatically. This lexicon can be used for further ASR or TTS system development. In addition to this phonetization task, we also developed a second lexicon using one of the P2P modules from previous experiments as explained in section 4.3. We chose the P2P that contains 1000 phoneme pairs (Malay-Iban phonemes) to phonetize only pure Iban words and we kept Malay G2P to phonetize Malay-Iban common words.

As a final evaluation, we post-edited 2000 random outputs taken from both lexicon. In this random set, there are 1426 pure Iban words and 574 Malay-Iban common words. The random outputs scored at 8.1% PER and 29.4% WER based on the G2P strategy, whereas the results from the P2P strategy are 10.2% PER and 38.1% WER.

Compared to our previous experimental results as shown in Table 5, our strategy to phonetize the Iban lexicon using G2Ps actually gave favourable outputs. Although the error rates are not the lowest, they are also not the worst. The PER falls in the range between 6.52% (Malay G2P score) and 8.2% (Iban G2P score) and WER in between 27.2% and 31.8%. Unfortunately, the P2P strategy returned lower accuracy values compared to the G2P strategy results. Table 6 presents a summary of the Malay and Iban phonetizers and their performances. In summary, the Iban G2P and P2P performances on Iban lexicon are a little worse than those of Malay G2P on Malay test set (6.2% PER; see Section 2.1).

5 Conclusions and future work

In this paper, we described the language contact between a local dominant language Malay and an under-resourced language from the same family, Iban. This study involved the comparison of

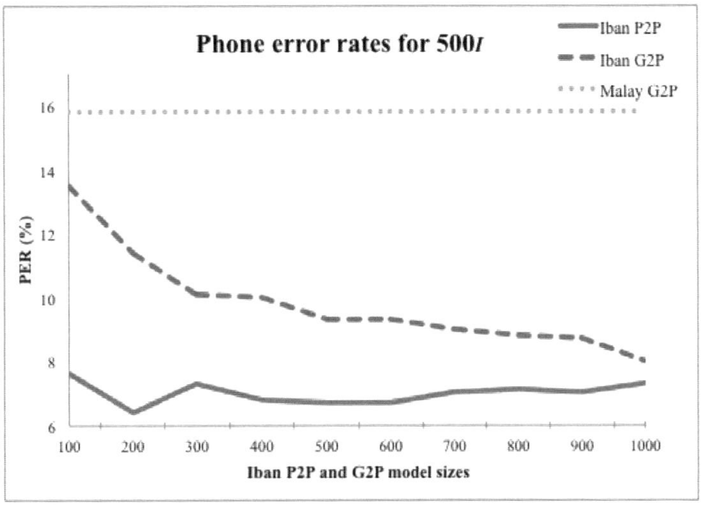

Figure 1: Phonetization results for 500 pure Iban words (*I*) obtained by employing different sizes of G2P and P2P models. Malay G2P (round dots) result is also plotted on the graph as our baseline study.

Phonetizer	#words	PER	WER
Malay G2P	8050 (Malay)	6.2	24.98
Iban G2P	2000 (Iban)	8.1	29.4
Iban P2P		10.2	38.1

Table 6: *Performance of Malay and Iban phonetizers. Measurement based on percentage (%)*.

Malay and Iban phonemes and pronunciation distance measurement on Malay-Iban common surface forms using the Levenshtein distance method. Due to our findings on the Malay-Iban connection, we built our first Iban G2P using post-edited Malay G2P output which, was done in less than 2 hours of manual post-editing by a native speaker.

Our preliminary results on two testing sets revealed that the two phonetizers, Malay and Iban G2Ps, are necessary to handle different word groups (Malay-Iban or pure Iban words). Thus, both Malay and Iban G2Ps were used in our attempt to produce the first Iban pronunciation lexicon. Besides that, we also employed Malay G2P and Iban P2P as our second strategy to obtain the lexicon.

To compare sample outputs with the post-edited list, we selected 2000 random phoneme sequences from the G2P and P2P outputs. We discovered that the G2P (results : 8.1% PER and 29.4% WER) is more accurate than the P2P. However, both Iban G2P and P2P performed lower than the Malay G2P.

As a continuation work on Iban phonetizers, our next research focus will be on tying Malay G2P and Iban P2P as a potential way to reduce the "knowledge gap" between Malay and Iban pronunciations. At the moment, the Malay G2P suits better for phonetizing Malay-Iban common words. While results on 2000 sample outputs from the Iban lexicon are not in favour of Iban P2P, the phonetizer did give higher accuracies compared to G2P phonetizers in our initial testings on pure Iban words. Hence, a suitable tying approach such as weighted finite states transducers, for example, could probably improve our phonetizer's accuracy. Besides that, our future goal is to build an Iban ASR system using Malay acoustic models and our new Iban pronunciation lexicon.

References

Sarawak Education-Department, 2007. *Sistem Jaku Iban di Sekula*. Sarawak, Malaysia, 1st edition.

W. Heeringa and F. de Wet. 2008. The origin of afrikaans pronunciation: a comparison to west germanic languages and dutch dialects. In *Proceedings of Conference of the Pattern Recognition Association of South Africa*, pages 159–164.

V. I. Levenshtein. 1966. Binary codes capable of correcting deletions, insertions and reversals. In *Soviet Physics-Doklady*, volume 10, pages 707–710.

M. P. Lewis, Gary F. Simons, and Charles D. Fennig. 2013. Ethnologue : Languages of the world, sil international. available at : http://www.ethnologue.com.

Y. M. Maris. 1979. *The Malay Sound System*. Siri Teks Fajar Bakti, Kuala Lumpur.

Ee Lee Ng, Alvin Wee Yeo, and Bali Ranaivo-Malançon. 2009. Identification of closely-related indigenous languages:an orthographic approach. In *Proc. of International Conference on Asian Language Processing.*, number 230-235. IEEE.

NIST. 2010. Speech recognition scoring toolkit (sctk). available at : http://www.nist.gov/speech/tools/.

Josef R. Novak. 2012. Phonetisaurus: A wfst-driven phoneticizer. available at : https://code.google.com/p/phonetisaurus.

Asmah Haji Omar. 1981. Phonology. In *The Iban Language of Sarawak*, pages 16–41, Kuala Lumpur, Malaysia. Dewan Bahasa dan Pustaka.

Bali Rainavo-Malançon. 2004. Computational analysis of affixed words in malay language. In *Internal Publication, Universiti Sains Malaysia.*

Malaysian Statistics-Department. 2010. Negeri sarawak:total population by ethnic group, subdistrict and state. Technical report, Statistics Department, Malaysia.

Andreas Stolcke. 2002. Srilm - an extensible language modeling toolkit. In *Proc. of the 7th International Conference on Spoken Language Processing (ICSLP 2002)*, pages 901–904.

Morris Swadesh. 1952. Lexico-statistic dating of prehistoric ethnic contacts. In *Proc. of the American Philosophical Society*, volume 96, pages 452–463.

T. P. Tan, H. Li, E. K. Tang, X. Xiao, and E. S. Chng. 2009. Mass: a malay language lvsr corpus resource. In *Proc. of 2009 Oriental COCOSDA International Conference*, pages 26–30.

LexToPlus: A Thai Lexeme Tokenization and Normalization Tool

Choochart Haruechaiyasak and Alisa Kongthon
Speech and Audio Technology Laboratory (SPT)
National Electronics and Computer Technology Center (NECTEC)
Thailand Science Park, Klong Luang, Pathumthani 12120, Thailand
{choochart.har, alisa.kon}@nectec.or.th

Abstract

The increasing popularity of social media has a large impact on the evolution of language usage. The evolution includes the transformation of some existing terms to enhance the expression of the writer's emotion and feeling. Text processing tasks on social media texts have become much more challenging. In this paper, we propose *LexToPlus*, a Thai lexeme tokenizer with term normalization process. LexToPlus is designed to handle the intentional errors caused by the repeated characters at the end of words. LexToPlus is a dictionary-based parser which detects existing terms in a dictionary. Unknown tokens with repeated characters are merged and removed. We performed statistical analysis and evaluated the performance of the proposed approach by using a Twitter corpus. The experimental results show that the proposed algorithm yields an accuracy of 96.3% on a test data set. The errors are mostly caused by the out-of-vocabulary problem which can be solved by adding newly found terms into the dictionary.

1 Introduction

Thailand is among the top countries having a large population on social networking websites such as *Facebook* and *Twitter*. The recent statistics show that the number of social media users in Thailand has reached 18 millions (approximately 25% of the total population) as of the first quarter of 2013[1]. In addition to the enormous amount of texts being created daily, another challenging issue is the language usage on social media is much different from the traditional and formal language. Social media texts include chat message, SMS, comments and posts. These texts are usually short and noisy, i.e., contain some ill-formed, out-of-vocabulary, abbreviated, transliterated and homophonic transformed terms. These special characteristics are due to many reasons including inconvenience in typing on virtual keyboards of smartphones and intentional transformation of existing terms to better express the emotion and feeling of the writers. As a result, performing basic text processing tasks such as term tokenization has become much more challenging.

Tokenizing Thai written texts is more difficult than languages in which word boundary markers are placed between words. Thai language is considered as an unsegmented language in which words are written continuously without the use of word delimiters. Word segmentation is considered a basic yet very important NLP task in many unsegmented languages. The main goal of word segmentation task is to assign correct word boundaries on given text strings. Previous approaches applied to Thai word segmentation can be broadly classified as *dictionary-based* and *machine learning*. The dictionary-based approach relies on a set of terms from a dictionary for parsing and segmenting input texts into word tokens. During the parsing process, series of characters are looked up on the dictionary for matching terms. The performance of the dictionary-based approach depends on the quality and size of the word set in the dictionary. Recent works in Thai word segmentation have adopted machine learning algorithms. The machine learning approach relies on a model trained from a corpus by using sequential labeling algorithms. Using the annotated corpus in which word boundaries are explicitly marked with a special character, the algorithm could be applied to train a model based on the features (e.g., character types) surrounding these boundaries.

[1]Zocial Inc. blog, *http://blog.zocialinc.com/thailand-zocial-award-2013-summary/*

The errors caused during the tokenization process can be categorized into two classes, *unintentional* and *intentional*. The unintentional errors are the typographical errors caused by careless typing (Peterson, 1980; Brill and Moore., 2000). This type of errors has been rigorously studied in the area of word editing and optical character recognition (OCR). There are three cases of typographical errors: *insertion*, *deletion* and *transposition*. Insertion error is caused by additional characters in a word. Deletion error is caused by missing characters in a word. Transposition error are caused by swapping of characters in the adjacent positions. Table 1 shows some examples of Thai word errors for all cases. The correct spellings are shown in parentheses with translations.

Unintentional Spelling error	Example
(1) Insertion	ข้าสว (ข้าว = rice)
(2) Deletion	หน้ต่าง (หน้าต่าง = window)
(3) Transposition	ทำงนา (ทำงาน = work)

Table 1: Unintentional spelling error types and examples

The scope of this paper does not include the unintentional errors which have been well studied. Instead we focus on intentional errors, i.e., words in which users intentionally create and type. Based on our preliminary study, the intentional errors can be classified into four categories: *insertion*, *transformation*, *transliteration* and *onomatopoeia*. The intentional insertion error is caused by typing repeated characters at the end of a word to emphasize the emotion or feeling. The transformation error is caused by alteration of existing terms and can be categorized into two subtypes: *homophonic* and *syllable trimming*. The homophonic terms refer to terms with the same or similar pronunciation to existing terms. The syllable trimming is a transformed term by deleting one or more syllables from an existing term for the purpose of reducing the keystrokes. The transliterated terms are created by using the Thai character set to create new terms from other languages. The last intentional error is the onomatopoeia terms which are created to phonetically imitate various sounds.

In this paper, we propose a solution for tokenizing and normalizing texts with the intentional insertion errors, i.e., users insert repeated characters at the end of words. The statistics on a 2-million Twitter corpus show that this type of errors accounts for approximately 4.8% of corpus size. Our proposed method is a longest matching dictionary-based approach with a rule-based normalization process. From our initial evaluation, the dictionary-based approach can handle the case of repeated characters better than the machine-learning based. More analysis and discussion will be given in the paper.

The remainder of this paper is organized as follows. In next section, we review some related works in word segmentation, text tokenization and term normalization for both segmented and unsegmented languages. In Section 3, we first give a formal definition of the tokenization task. Then we present the proposed algorithm for implementing LexToPlus. In Section 4, we give the performance evaluation by using a data set collected from Twitter. Some examples of errors are presented with some discussion. Section 5 concludes the paper with the future work.

2 Related work

Many techniques for word segmentation and morphological analysis have been reported for unsegmented languages. Peng et al. applied the linear-chain CRFs model for Chinese word segmentation (Peng et al., 2004). Their proposed model included a probabilistic new word detection method to further improve the performance. For Thai word segmentation, many previous works also applied machine learning algorithms to train the models. Meknavin et al. combined the model of word segmentation with the POS tagging (Meknavin et al., 1997). Their proposed model solved the ambiguity problem by using a feature-based model. Kruengkrai and Isahara applied the CRFs to train a word segmentation model for Thai language (Kruengkrai and Isahara, 2006). Two path selection schemes based on confidence estimation and Viterbi were proposed to solve the ambiguity problem. Haruechaiyasak et al. compared the performance among the dictionary-based approach and many machine learning techniques such as CRFs and the Support Vector Machines (SVMs) (Haruechaiyasak et al., 2008). The CRFs model was reported to outperform the dictionary-based approach and other machine learning algorithms.

While the majority of previous works focused on formal written texts, some works in text to-

	0	1	2	3	4	5	6	7	8	9	A	B	C	D	E	F
U+0E0x		ก	ข	ฃ	ค	ฅ	ฆ	ง	จ	ฉ	ช	ซ	ฌ	ญ	ฎ	ฏ
U+0E1x	ฐ	ฑ	ฒ	ณ	ด	ต	ถ	ท	ธ	น	บ	ป	ผ	ฝ	พ	ฟ
U+0E2x	ภ	ม	ย	ร	ฤ	ล	ฦ	ว	ศ	ษ	ส	ห	ฬ	อ	ฮ	ฯ
U+0E3x	ะ	ั	า	ำ	ิ	ี	ึ	ื	ุ	ู	ฺ					฿
U+0E4x	เ	แ	โ	ใ	ไ	ๅ	ๆ	็	่	้	๊	๋	์	ํ	๎	๏
U+0E5x	๐	๑	๒	๓	๔	๕	๖	๗	๘	๙	๚	๛				

Figure 1: Thai Unicode Characters

kenization have expanded the scope into real-world texts which often contains many out-of-vocabulary terms. Tokenization for short and noisy texts requires an additional process of text normalization. Early works for text normalization were focused on news text, newsgroups posts and classified ads. Sprout et al. performed a study on non-standard words (NSWs), including numbers, abbreviations, dates, currency amounts and acronyms (Sprout et al., 2001). They applied several techniques including n-gram language models, decision trees and weighted finite-state transducers and showed that the machine learning approaches yielded better performance than the rule-based approach.

More recent works in text normalization focused on real world texts which contain informal language, such as SMS, chat and social media. Aw et al. proposed an approach for normalizing SMS texts for machine translation task (Aw et al., 2006). The normalization task is viewed as a translation problem from the SMS language to the English language. The results showed that normalizing SMS texts before performing translation significantly improved the performance based on the BLEU score. Costa-Jussa and Banchs proposed an approach for normalizing short texts, i.e., SMS (Costa-Jussa and Banchs, 2013). The proposed approach adopted the idea from statistical machine translation (SMT) by combining statistical and rule-based techniques.

Han et al. proposed a classification-based approach to detect ill-formed words, and generates correction candidates based on morphophonemic similarity (Han and Baldwin, 2011; Han et al., 2013). The proposed approach was evaluated on both SMS and Twitter corpus. The best performance was achieved with the combination of dictionary lookup, word similarity and context support modelling. Hirst and Budanitsky proposed a method for detecting and correcting spelling errors (Hirst and Budanitsky, 2005). The proposed method is based on the identification of tokens that are semantically unrelated to their context. The method also detects tokens which are spelling variations of words that would be related to the context. Liu et al. identified and distinguished nonstandard tokens found in social media texts as intentionally and unintentionally (Liu et al., 2012). A normalization system was proposed by integrating different techniques including the enhanced letter transformation, visual priming, and string/phonetic similarity. The proposed system was evaluated on SMS and Twitter data sets. The results showed that the proposed system achieved over 90% word-coverage across all data sets.

Another related research is the study of onomatopoeia in which terms are created to phonetically imitate different sounds. Research in onomatopoeia has recently gained much attention for Japanese language. Asaga et al. presented an online onomatopoeia example-based dictionary called ONOMATOPEDIA (Asaga et al., 2008). The proposed approach includes the extraction and clustering of sentences containing onomatopoeias as learning examples. Uchida et al. studied some Japanese onomatopoeias which contain various emotions (Uchida et al., 2001). Users are asked to rate emotion in each onomatopoeia. Correct identification of emotion from onomatopoeia could be used in advanced semantic analysis. Kato et al. proposed an approach to extract onomatopoeia found in food reviews (Kato et al., 2012). The extracted onomatopoeia terms can help users search for food or restaurants. In Thai language, many onomatopoeia terms are found in chat and social media texts. We classify onomatopoeia as another type of intentional errors while performing tokenization. Details are given and discussed in later section of the paper.

Intentional Spelling error	Example
(1) Insertion	มากกกกก (มาก = very) โอ๊ยยยยย (โอ๊ย = ouch!) ว้าววววว (ว้าว = wow) แล้วววววว (แล้ว = already)
(2) Transformation	
(2.1) Homophonic	มั่ก (มาก = very) เด๋ว (เดี๋ยว = just) ร้าก (รัก = love) อะเคร (โอเค = okay) เมิง (มึง = you) กรู (กู = I) e-ngo (อีโง่ = idiot) จุงเบย (จังเลย = really) 555 (ฮ่าๆๆ = ha ha ha)
(2.2) Syllable trimming	มหาลัย (มหาวิทยาลัย = university) โอ (โอเค = okay) มอไซค์ (มอเตอร์ไซค์ = motorcycle) เตี๋ยว (ก๋วยเตี๋ยว = noodle)
(3) Transliteration	นอย (พารานอยด์ = paranoid) ชิว ชิว (chill chill)
(4) Onomatopoeia	แง (baby crying sound) ตู้ม (explosion sound) จุ๊บ (kissing sound) เอี๊ยด (braking sound)

Table 2: Intentional spelling error types and examples

3 Tokenization and normalization for Thai texts

Thai language has its own set of characters or alphabets. It has 44 consonants, 15 vowel symbols and four tone marks. Consonants are written horizontally from left to right, with vowels placed in four positions: above, below, left and right of the corresponding consonant. Tone marks can be placed in the position above of consonants and some vowels. There are 87 valid characters in Unicode system (shown in Figure 1).

3.1 Problem definition

The problem of tokenization for unsegmented languages can be defined as follows. Given a string of *N* words, $w_0 w_1 \ldots w_{N-1}$, each word w_i consists of a series of characters, $c_0^i c_1^i \ldots c_{|w_i|-1}^i$, where $|w_i|$ is the number of characters in w_i. The tokenization task is to assign a word boundary between two words, e.g., $w_i|w_j$, where | represents a word boundary character.

From our preliminary study, the errors from tokenizing Thai texts from social media texts are due to four cases: insertion, transformation, transliteration and onomatopoeia. These error types are considered as *intentional errors* as opposed to the unintentional errors previously mentioned. Intentional errors are caused by users intentionally create, alter and transform existing words on different purposes. Table 2 lists all error types with some examples. The original terms or brief descriptions are shown in parentheses with translations. Each error type is fully explained as follows.

1. **Insertion**: This type of error is caused by repeated characters at the end of a word. Using the above problem definition, the error can be described as follows, $c_0^i c_1^i \ldots c_{|w_i|-1}^i c_{|w_i|-1}^i c_{|w_i|-1}^i c_{|w_i|-1}^i$, in which the last character $c_{|w_i|-1}^i$ is repeated more than once. This error type also appears in English, e.g., *whatttt*, *sleepyyy* and *loveeee*.

2. **Transformation**: This error type is caused by transformation of existing terms and can be categorized into two following types.

   Homophonic: The homophonic terms refer to terms with the same or similar pronunciation. A homophonic term is normally created by replacing an original vowel with a new vowel which has similar sound. Some examples in English are *luv (love)*, *kinda (kind of)* and *gal (girl).*

   Syllable trimming: The syllable trimming is a transformed term by deleting one or more syllables from an existing term for the purpose of reducing the keystrokes.

3. **Transliteration**: Thai Transliterated terms are newly created terms converted from other

language scripts. Transliterated terms are commonly found in modern Thai written texts, e.g., chat and social media. Most of the terms are transliterated from English terms including named entities such as company and product names.

4. **Onomatopoeia**: Thai onomatopoeia terms are created by using the Thai character set to form new terms to imitate different sounds in nature and environment including humans and animals. Onomatopoeia terms are typically used in chat and social media texts to make the communications between users more vivid. For example, to make the kissing action sound more realistic, the word *joob* in Thai (or *smooch* in English) which imitates the kissing sound is normally used.

3.2 The proposed solution

To select an appropriate approach for tokenizing and normalizing social media texts, we first perform a comparison between two approaches, dictionary-based (DCB) and machine learning based (MLB) (Haruechaiyasak et al., 2008). For machine learning based approach, we adopt the conditional random fields (CRFs) algorithm to train the tokenization model. The dictionary-based approach is a lexicon-based parser which solves the ambiguity with a longest matching heuristic. Table 3 shows tokenized results from different approaches. The input text consists of three words. Each word contains the insertion of some repeated characters at the end. The correct terms are bolded and underlined. The MLB approach cannot correctly assign the word boundaries between words. The first problem is due to the repeated characters at the end of each word. All repeated characters are recognized as part of the word. The second problem is due to the out-of-vocabulary which results in a word is incorrectly tokenized as two separating words.

The DCB approach can correctly tokenize all the terms which are included in the dictionary. The repeated word-ending characters are merged into a chunk. To further normalize the output words, we propose an algorithm DCB-Norm, which is a dictionary-based tokenization with a term normalization process. The DCB-Norm algorithm is shown in Figure 2. The algorithm performs text parsing with longest matching strategy (*LM_PARSE*). The strategy is used to solve the ambiguity problem in which there are more than one possible path to select in the parsing tree. The longest matching uses the heuristic such that longer terms contain better semantic than shorter terms. Figure 3 illustrates the dictionary-based tokenization with longest matching. From the example, there are four possible path to select. The longest matching strategy select the path (shown with a thick solid line) which contains a term with the largest length.

Input text: ง่วงงงงนอนนนนนจังเลยยยย

<table>
<tr><th>Approach</th><th>Tokenized results</th></tr>
<tr><td>MLB</td><td>|ง่วง|งงง|นอนนนนน|จัง|เลยยยย|</td></tr>
<tr><td>DCB</td><td>|ง่วง|งงง|นอน|นนนน|จังเลย|ยยย|</td></tr>
<tr><td>DCB-Norm</td><td>|ง่วง|นอน|จังเลย|</td></tr>
</table>

Table 3: An example of tokenized results

```
Algorithm: DCB-Norm (input_text)
Input: A set of N terms, T, from dictionary
Output: tokenized_text
load T into TRIE data structure
while (not end of string)
    token, token_type ← LM_PARSE (input_text, TRIE)
    if (token_type equal to unknown)
        if (token not equal repeated characters)
            merge unknown token into chunk
            append (chunk + |) to tokenized_text
    else
        append (token + |) to tokenized_text
return tokenized_text
```

Note: | denotes a word boundary marker

Figure 2: DCB-Norm algorithm

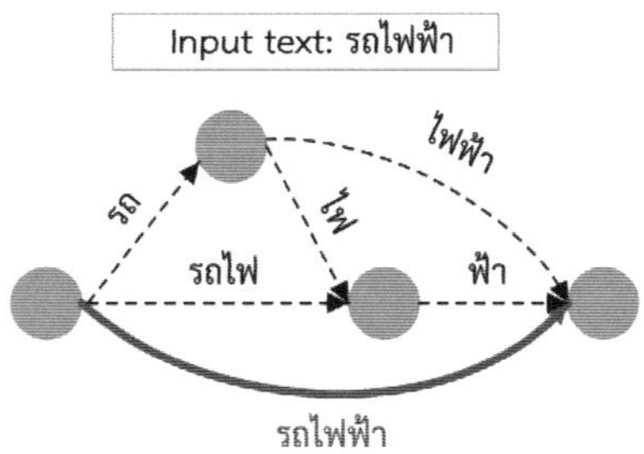

Figure 3: An example of tokenizing parse tree.

A set of terms in a lexicon is stored in a trie, an efficient data structure in terms of storage space and retrieval time (Frakes and Baeza-Yates, 1992). Figure 4 illustrates a trie storing an example set of terms. The algorithm begins by parsing the input text. A chunk of characters are looked up with terms stored in TRIE. If the character chunk are not found in TRIE and consists of same characters, it will be neglected. On the other hand, if a character chunk is found in TRIE, a word boundary marker (denoted with |) will be assigned at the end of the chunk.

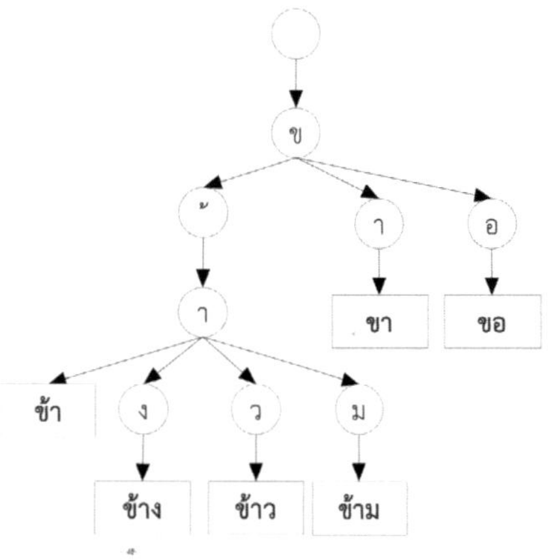

Figure 4: An example of trie

4 Experiments and discussion

In this section, we first perform a statistical analysis on a Twitter corpus to observe language usage characteristics. An experiment is then performed to evaluate the proposed tokenization and normalization solution.

4.1 Statistical analysis

To understand the characteristics of the language usage among Thai users on Twitter, we analyze a Twitter corpus consisting of *2,388,649* posts in Thai language. The total number of all words in the corpus is *25,683,296*. The number of unique tokens in the corpus is equal to *81,136*.

We run the *DCB-Norm* algorithm on the corpus and collect all repeated character chunks. Table 4 summarizes statistics of number of grams in repeated word-ending characters. Figure 5 shows the plot of the gram statistics. It can be observed that the occurrence of repeated characters is gradually decreased with the number of grams. From the corpus, we observe that some of the

# repeated grams	# posts
1	39,986
2	27,315
3	18,069
4	9,820
5	5,270
6 or more	14,560
Total	**115,020**

Table 4: Number of grams in repeated characters

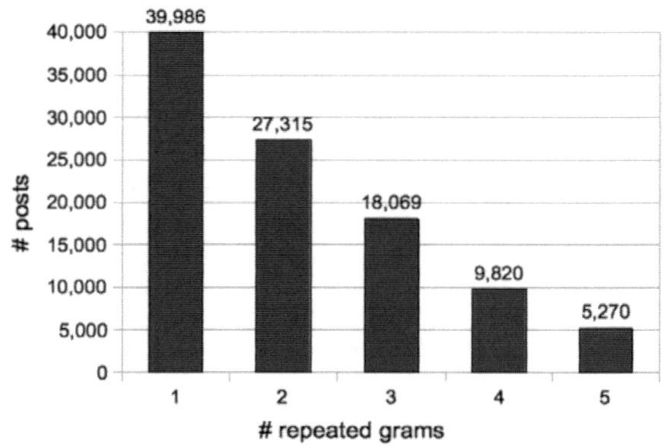

Figure 5: Number of grams in repeated characters

แล้ว (10291)	กรี๊ด (2774)	แว้ว (2061)
เนี่ย (1921)	โอ้ว (1810)	โว้ย (1387)
อืม (1142)	สาด (1124)	เว้ย (935)
เล้ย (896)	แร้ว (875)	อิ้ว (790)
แย้ว (789)	ยอด (787)	เลย (786)
โอย (751)	ข้าว (734)	เรย (720)
โอ๊ย (706)	หิว (682)	โอ้ย (666)
ด้วย (615)	ว้อย (613)	ว้าว (602)
เฮ้ย (574)	นอน (563)	แสรด (533)

Table 5: Top ranked terms with repeated characters

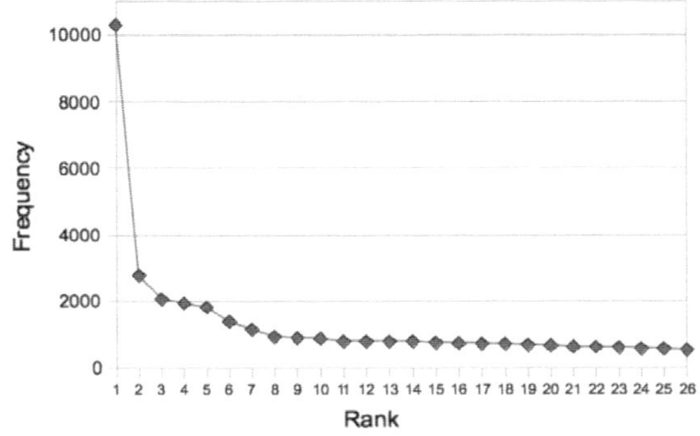

Figure 6: Top ranked terms with repeated characters

posts containing more than 10 repeated character grams. Another observation is the repeated characters mostly occur at the end of the words as we expected.

Next, we analyze the high frequent terms which contains the repeated characters. Table 5 shows top ranked terms with repeated characters. The total number of posts which contain some repeated characters is 115,020 which is equal to 4.8% of corpus size. Figure 6 shows the plot of top ranked terms. From the figure, we observe the Zipf (or long-tail) distribution over the terms with repeated characters. Most of the top terms are very informal and often used in conversational language. Some of the terms are used to express the feeling and emotion of the users.

4.2 Experiments and discussion

To evaluate the performance of the proposed approach, we perform an experiment by using a set of 1,000 randomly selected Twitter posts written in Thai language. Each post contains some repeated characters and is manually assigned with correct word boundary markers. For the proposed DCB-Norm algorithm, we use a lexicon from LEX*i*TRON[2] which contains *35,328* general terms. We also include another lexicon consisting of *1,341* terms frequently found in Twitter corpus. Words obtained from Twitter lexicon include chat, slangs and transliterated words from other languages.

The performance evaluation is carried out on a notebook with a 2 GHz Intel Core 2 Duo CPU, 4 GB RAM running under Mac OS X. We evaluate the algorithm in terms of accuracy, i.e., the number of correctly tokenized texts over the total number of test texts. We also evaluate the running time efficiency. The results are summarized in Table 6. The overall accuracy is equal to *96.3%*. To analyze the errors, we manually look at the incorrectly tokenized results. We observe that in the case of all words in the text are in the dictionary, the words are recognized and the repeated characters are correctly removed. However, the problem is mostly due to out-of-vocabulary (OOV) which causes the incorrect assignment of word boundary markers. As a result, the words with repeated characters at the end could be not normalized correctly. Two error types associated with OOV problem is homophonic transformation and transliteration. Table 7 shows some examples from the error analysis. The simplest solution to the OOV problem is to manually collect newly created terms from the corpus.

Accuracy	96.3%
Average Throughput	435,596 words/sec

Table 6: Evaluation results

<table>
<tr><th>Error type</th><th>Example</th></tr>
<tr><td>Homophonic transformation</td><td>|โอ๊|ววว| |แม่เจ้า|
|หร่|อย|ยยย|
|ขอ|โท|ดดดดด|</td></tr>
<tr><td>Transliteration</td><td>|แซ|ฟฟ|ร่อน| (saffron)
|วู๊|ดดดดด| (Wood)
|อิ|ตา|เลี่ยน|นนนน (Italian)</td></tr>
</table>

Table 7: Examples of tokenized errors

5 Conclusion and future work

We proposed a tool called *LexToPlus* for tokenizing and normalizing Thai written texts. LexToPlus is designed to handle the intentional word errors commonly found in social media texts. In this paper, we focus on solving the tokenization errors caused by repeated characters at the end of words. The proposed algorithm DCB-Norm is a dictionary-based parser with a rule-based extension to merge and remove repeated characters. We

[2] LEX*i*TRON, *http://lexitron.nectec.or.th*

performed some statistical analysis on a Twitter corpus consisting of over 2 million posts written in Thai language. One interesting result is the ranking distribution of top terms with repeated characters follows the Zipf or long-tail distribution. We evaluated the proposed algorithm by using a corpus of 1,000 manually tokenized texts. The accuracy is equal to 96.3% with the average throughput of 435,596 words/second.

From the error analysis, we found that the major problem is the out-of-vocabulary (OOV) which comes from homophonic transformation and transliteration. Although the OOV problem can be partially solved by adding new terms into the dictionary. However, it is labor intensive and ineffective in long terms. For future work, we plan to improve the performance of the proposed algorithm by constructing a machine learning model to automatically detect new terms based on the contextual information.

References

Chisato Asaga, Yusuf Mukarramah and Chiemi Watanabe. 2008. ONOMATOPEDIA: onomatopoeia online example dictionary system extracted from data on the web. *Proc. of the 10th Asia-Pacific web conf. on Progress in WWW research and development* , 601-612.

AiTi Aw, Min Zhang, Juan Xiao, and Jian Su. 2006. A phrase-based statistical model for SMS text normalization. *Proc. of the COLING/ACL on Main conference poster sessions*, 33–40.

Eric Brill and Robert C. Moore. 2000. An improved error model for noisy channel spelling correction. *Proc. of the 38th Annual Meeting on Association for Computational Linguistics*, 286–293.

Marta R. Costa-Jussa and Rafael E. Banchs. 2013. Automatic normalization of short texts by combining statistical and rule-based techniques. *Language Resources and Evaluation* , 47(1):179–193.

William B. Frakes and Ricardo Baeza-Yates (Eds.). 1992. *Information Retrieval: Data Structures and Algorithms* , Prentice-Hall, Englewood Cliffs, NJ.

Bo Han and Timothy Baldwin. 2011. Lexical normalisation of short text messages: makn sens a #twitter. *Proc. of the 49th Annual Meeting of the Association for Computational Linguistics*, 368–378.

Bo Han, Paul Cook, and Timothy Baldwin. 2013. Lexical normalization for social media text. *ACM Transactions on Intelligent Systems and Technology*, 4(1): 1–27.

Choochart Haruechaiyasak, Sarawoot Kongyoung and Matthew Dailey. 2008. A comparative study on Thai word segmentation approaches. *Proc. of the ECTI-CON 2008*, 1:125-128.

Graeme Hirst and Alexander Budanitsky. 2005. Correcting real-word spelling errors by restoring lexical cohesion. *Natural Language Engineering*, 11:87–111.

Ayumi Kato, Yusuke Fukazawa, Tomomasa Sato and Taketoshi Mori. 2012. Extraction of onomatopoeia used for foods from food reviews and its application to restaurant search. *Proc. of the 21st int. conf. companion on World Wide Web* , 719-728.

Canasai Kruengkrai and Hitoshi Isahara. 2006. A conditional random field framework for thai morphological analysis. *Proc. of the Fifth Int. Conf. on Language Resources and Evaluation (LREC-2006).*

Fei Liu, Fuliang Weng, and Xiao Jiang. 2012. A broad-coverage normalization system for social media language. *Proc. of the 50th Annual Meeting of the Association for Computational Linguistics*, 1035-1044.

Surapant Meknavin, Paisarn Charoenpornsawat, and Boonserm Kijsirikul. 1997. Feature-Based Thai Word Segmentation. *Proc. of the Natural Language Processing Pacific Rim Symposium*, 289–296.

Fuchun Peng, Fangfang Feng, and Andrew McCallum. 2004. Chinese Segmentation and New Word Detection Using Conditional Random Fields. *Proc. of the 20th COLING*, 562–568.

James L. Peterson. 1980. Computer programs for detecting and correcting spelling errors. *Communications of ACM*, 23:676–687.

Richard Sproat, Alan W. Black, Stanley Chen, Shankar Kumar, Mari Ostendorf, and Christopher Richards. 2001. Normalization of non-standard words. *Computer Speech and Language*, 15(3):287 333.

Yuzu Uchida, Kenji Araki, and Jun Yoneyama. 2012. Classification of Emotional Onomatopoeias Based on Questionnaire Surveys. *Proc. of the 2012 International Conference on Asian Language Processing*, 1–4.

A Three-Layer Architecture for Automatic Post-Editing System Using Rule-Based Paradigm

Mahsa Mohaghegh
Unitec
Auckland, New Zealand
mmohaghegh@unitec.ac.nz

Abdolhossein Sarrafzadeh
Unitec
Auckland, New Zealand
hsarrafzadeh@unitec.ac.nz

Mehdi Mohammadi
SheikhBahaee University
Isfahan, Iran
mehdi.mka@gmail.com

Abstract

This paper proposes a post-editing model in which our three-level rule-based automatic post-editing engine called Grafix is presented to refine the output of machine translation systems. The type of corrections on sentences varies from lexical transformation to complex syntactical rearrangement. The experimental results both in manual and automatic evaluations show that the proposed system is able to improve the quality of our state-of-the-art English-Persian SMT system.

1 Introduction

The overall success of well-designed statistical machine translation (SMT) systems has made SMT one of the most popular machine translation (MT) approaches (Callison-Burch, Koehn, Monz, & Zaidan, 2011). Currently however, MT output is often seriously grammatically incorrect. This is more often the case in SMT than other approaches due to the absence of linguistic rules for the language pair on which it is being applied. Grammatical error not only weakens the fluency of the translation, but in certain cases it completely changes the meaning of a sentence. In morphologically rich languages, grammatical accuracy is of more significance, as the interpretation of syntactic relations depends heavily on morphological agreements within the sentences. Since our system's approach is SMT, and deals with Persian, a morphologically rich language, post-editing the output is an important step in maintaining the fluency of the translation, and as we will show, this can yield to higher evaluation scores and more fluent translation. Due to the repetitive nature of machine translation mistakes (Allen & Hogan, 2000) and the similarity of automatic post-editing (APE) process to machine translation process (Simard, Goutte, & Isabelle, 2007) certain MT systems can carry out the task of an APE component.

The SMT approach to MT is useful in that it operates on numerical data extracted from parallel corpus. This approach tends to reduce human cost at translation stage. However, the search cost is expensive, and the system has no linguistic background (although generally it is this that enables the system to be applied to any language pair after training on language-specific data). Most systems of this approach also encounter difficulties when capturing long distance phenomena.

RBMT approaches are categorized under three different types: Direct Systems, Transfer RBMT Systems that employ morphological and syntactical analysis, and Interligual RBMT Systems that use an abstract meaning. The Grafix APE system follows the pattern of Transfer-based systems. The aim of development of Grafix system is to correct some grammatical SMT system errors frequently occur in English-to-Persian translations.

2 Related Works

According to Xuan, Li, and Tang (2011) the most popular combinations of MT systems and APE modules are a RBMT main system linked with phrase-based SMT (PB-SMT) and a RBMT main system linked with Example-based MT (EBMT). Simard et al. (2007) and Lagarda, Alabau, Casacuberta, Silva, and Diaz-de-Liano (2009) and Isabelle, Goutte, and Simard (2007) have used a phrase-based SMT to enhance the output of an RBMT system. Pilevar (2011), in his recent work used a statistical post-editing (SPE) approach to improve the translation of subtitles for movies for the English-Persian language pair. The author notes that in contrast to same reported experiments in other languages, their result for the combination of RBMT+SPE is slightly weaker than SMT alone.

Ahsan, Kolachina, Kolachina, Sharma, and Sangal (2010) document work using a modular RBMT system which is able to combine the two translation approaches at different stages in the RBMT system's pipeline. In this way, exploration of rules for both local and long distance reordering could be performed independently, and such reordering leading to improved translation output could be identified and utilized. In their paper, the authors show an increase in the output score for each stage of combination.

Recently however, there has been more interest in the use of RBMT as the base for an APE system. Marecek, Rosa, and Bojar (2011) report their experiments in correcting the output of an English-Czech MT system. They performed a rule-based grammatical correction module, DEPFIX, on sentences parsed to dependency trees. Their baseline SMT system relies on Moses, a phrase-based translation system. Their two-step translation is a setup in which the English source is translated into simplified Czech. Then the simplified Czech is monotonically transferred to a fully inflected Czech. In 2012, Rosa, Marecek, and Du˘sek (2012) enhanced DEPFIX by enriching the rule set and using a modified version of MST Parser. These two modifications, based on their results, led to higher scores.

3 Description of the System

In this study, we couple the PeEn-SMT system previously developed by Mohaghegh, Sarrafzadeh, and Moir (2011) with an RBMT-based APE. The architecture of our system differs from common approaches like Simard, et al. (2007) and Lagarda, et, al. (2009). Because of its use of language and translation models over large corpora, together with better lexical selection, SMT would be capable of consistently providing fluent translation. This approach, however, lacks linguistic knowledge, which we believe is more important when it comes to an APE. In this area we believe RBMT is a superior base due to its strengths in linguistic knowledge.

Three levels of transformations as shown in Figure 1, constitute the overal design of the Transfer-based APE module: lexical transformers, shallow transformers and deep transformers. The output of the SMT system is passed to the APE as input. This is then run through a series of transformers and fine-tuned in an effort to achieve a more accurate translation.

3.1 The Underlying SMT System

Persian is a morphologically rich language, so word disordering is a common issue that we face. Hierarchical SMT (D. Chiang, 2005) as an extension to phrase-based translation takes syntax into account to some extent, with phrases being used to learn word reordering. This improvement is due to the word order differences between Persian and English, which are better handled with a hierarchical phrase based system than a standard phrase-based approach. These advantages of hierarchical SMT encouraged us to conduct our study on Joshua after numerous experiments with Moses.

Hierarchical phrase-based translation allows phrases with gaps to be modeled as synchronous context-free grammars (SCFGs). In effect, it is grammars that are used, not phrase tables. The hierarchical approach does not detract from the strengths of phrase-based approaches, but uses them to its advantage. Phrases are used in order to learn word reordering. In a hierarchical approach, this principle is taken a step further, and phrases are used for *phrase* reordering, using SCFGs to compose the hierarchical phrases from words and sub-phrases and represent translation models.
Joshua (Li, Callison-Burch, Khudanpur, & Thornton, 2009), a hierarchical phrase based machine translation toolkit, was a reimplementation of the Hiero MT system (D. Chiang, 2007), and is able to support formalisms such as SAMT

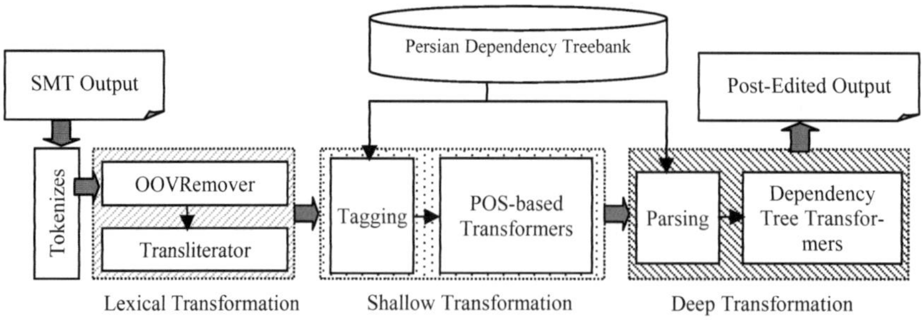

Figure 1. Overall architecture of the proposed Rule-based APE system

(Zollmann & Venugopal, 2006). More recent efforts introduced the Thrax module, an extensible Hadoop-based extraction toolkit for synchronous context free grammars (Weese, Ganitkevitch, Callison-Burch, Post, & Lopez, 2011).

In Joshua, an SCFG can be represented as a set of rules given as:

$$C_i \rightarrow <\alpha_i , \gamma_i , \sim_i , \varphi_i> \quad (1)$$

where C_i is a non-terminal symbol of the grammar, α_i and γ_i are sequences of terminal and non-terminal symbols for the source and target sides respectively, $\sim_i$ is a correspondence between the non-terminals of α_i and γ_i, and φ_i is a feature vector defining the probability of translation from α_i to γ_i.

3.2 Training Data Source

Grammatical relations may be represented by dependency structures. Compared to syntactic trees, dependency structures are more specific in regard to semantics rather than strict word order (Ambati, 2008). The structure of sentence dependency tree represents the relationship between words as either modifying or being modified, and the root in each tree being the only word which does not modify any other word.

The Persian Dependency Treebank[1], containing over 12500 sentences and 189000 tokens, is our main source of training data for POS-tagging and dependency parsing. Its data format is based on CoNLL Shared Task on Dependency Parsing (Buchholz & Marsi, 2006).

3.3 Pre-Processing and Tagging

We pre-process input Persian sentences using our implemented tokenizer component. It eliminates whitespace, semi-space, tab and new line in order to tokenize the text. We also considered punctuation marks in sentences in cases where punctuation marks were attached to other words.

POS-tagging the input text is a pre-requisite process for both shallow and deep transformation levels. The Maximum Likelihood Estimation (MLE) is the underlying algorithm in the POS-tagger component for our APE method and is trained with the Persian Dependency Treebank data. Evaluation showed that the use of this approach for tagging the Persian language yielded promising results (Raja et al., 2007). Tagging tests showed the best accuracy to be 95.43%.

3.4 Parsing

There has recently been increasing interest in the use of dependency models for a number of applications in NLP, particularly since certain characteristics of the dependency structure prove to be advantageous over other syntactic representations (Ding & Palmer, 2005). In a dependency parsing tree, words are linked to their arguments by dependency representations (Hudson, 1984).

We used an implementation of Dependency Parsing named MSTParser. MSTParser's main algorithm is Maximum Spanning Tree in which the maximum spanning tree should be found in order to find the best parse tree (Kübler, McDonald, & Nivre, 2009).

3.5 Three-Level Rule-based Transformers

We acquired translation rules manually by investigating a broad range of incorrect translations and determining frequent wrong patterns among them. In order to determine incorrect patterns and define correction rules for them, it is necessary to parse both the MT output and the reference text.

By investigating the incorrect and incomplete translation outputs and considering the dependency parser output for these sentences, a number of incorrect patterns were identified in the POS sequence and Dependency parse tree of these sentences. These patterns are compared against the Persian Dependency Treebank to ensure that they do not match a known correct sequence.

Lexical Transformation: Two components are serving in the first level of transformations. OOV[2] remover is a substitution rule like $E \rightarrow F_1, F_2 \ldots F_n$ where E is an English word and $F_i = F_1, F_2 \ldots F_n$ are different translations of the word in Persian. This rule replaces a remained English word in the MT output with the correct translation in Persian. Since no Word Sense Disambiguation (WSD) component is present, it is assumed that the first meaning found for the English word in the dictionary used is the most frequent translation of the word, so it is used as replacement for the English word. A transliterator also is used to complement the operation of OOV remover in cases that

[1] http://dadegan.ir/en

[2] Out Of Vocabulary

OOV remover could not find any equivalent Persian translation for English words in the output. A transliterator works based on training an amount of prepared data to produce the most likely Persian word for the English word remaining in the sentence. The result is the English word appearing composed with Persian character scripts. The training data set for transliterator contains over 4600 of the most frequently used Persian words and named entities written using English letters, and also the equivalent in Persian script. In order to implement the transliterator component we used some libraries from Virastyar[3] software.

Shallow Transformers: The second stage of the system involves a shallow transfer module which is based on some POS patterns identified as incorrect. Incorrect or incomplete POS sequence patterns will be controlled for each sentence, and appropriate rules executed to revise them. Description of some shallow rules comes in following section.

IncompleteDependentTransformer: Relative pronouns such as «که» in Persian (English *"that"*) which POS-tagged as SUBR, suggest continuation of the phrase by a dependent clause. If it occurred in a POS sequence without a consequent verb, an incomplete dependent sentence would be identified and a verb should complete the sentence. Currently, in most instances the verb «است» (English *"is"*) is suggested.

IncompleteEndedPREMTransformer: Pre-modifiers (denoted by PREM) are noun modifiers. According to the definition, modifiers should precede nouns, so a POS sequence in which a pre-modifier located at the end of a sentence deemed as incorrect. These sequences were removed from the sentence altogether since there is no logical translation for given input.

AdjectiveArrangementTransformer: In the Persian language, adjectives usually come after the nouns they describe. For instance (English *"heavy bag"*) «کیف سنگین» is translated literally as *"bag heavy"*. The only exception in this group is superlative adjectives, which are identified by the suffix «ترین» attached to the adjective. In this special case, the adjective comes before the noun to define it. The appearance of non-superlative adjectives before their described nouns indicates incorrect composition which must be corrected by this transformer.

Deep Transformers: In this type of transformations, the input is parsed by a dependency parser. Once the text is POS-tagged, some preparation is performed to parse the input, according to the parsing input format (McDonald, Pereira, Ribarov, & Hajic, 2005). The rules here examine dependency tree of each sentence to verify it bounds to some syntactical and grammatical constraints. The tree structure of each parsed sentence will be analyzed, and those sentences with incorrect parse tree structures will be evaluated to determine if correction is necessary. Some deep rules are described in sections below.

NoSubjectSentenceTransformer: Compared to known translation reference sentences, it was seen in some cases that what was parsed as the object in the sentence was actually the subject. Such sentences have a third person verb, no definite subject and an object tagged as POSTP (postposition) in the POS sequence. This transformer is designed to revise the sentence by removing the postposition «را» which is the indicator of a direct object in the sentence. Removal of this postposition changes the sentence to one with a subject.

PluralNounsTransformer: Unlike English, in the Persian language the word coming after a number is always singular. In SMT output there are instances where plural nouns are located after a number (< PRENUM> POS). This is corrected by removing the plural symbol of Persian words. The suffix«ها» (/hā/) is the most common plural indicator, which is removed in this rule.

VerbArrangementTransformer: Persian language has a preferred word order, with SOV (subject-object-verb) followed by SVO. These two types make up more than 75% of natural languages having a preferred order (Crystal, 2004) . Although reordering of sentence components does not necessarily lead to a significant change in meaning, there are many cases where these changes may disturb the fluency and accuracy of the sentence. One frequently occurring case is sentences in which a main verb as Root does not occur immediately before the period punctuation. The transformer treats such cases as follows: the sentence is

[3] http://sourceforge.net/projects/virastyar/

reordered by moving the root verb and its NVE[4] dependants (in the case of compound verbs) to the end of the sentence, just before the period punctuation mark.

MissingVerbTransformer: Sometimes sentences from SMT output can occur with missing verbs specifically in the case of compound verbs. We used the Persian [verb] Valency Lexicon (Rasooli, Moloodi, Kouhestani, & Minaei-Bidgoli, 2011) to determine the proper verb for a non-verbal element in the sentence. All obligatory and optional non-verbal elements (main-verb dependents) are listed in this lexicon. For example, the verb «مصرف کردن» (English *"to consume"*) is composed of two elements. Searching for «مصرف» in this lexicon will return «کردن» as the main part of that particular compound. We find the correct root of the verb (past or present) by examining the other verbs in a sentence which could show the correct tense intended for that sentence. The present tense is chosen by default if there are no other verbs in the sentence. Any subject with a referred verb preceding the subject in the dependency tree is identified as an incorrect linked subject to any verb due to violence of standard SOV structure. In this case, the last word in the sentence is considered as a candidate of non-verbal element in the Verb Valency Lexicon. If a corresponding verb is found, the correct tense of that verb will be inserted into the space of the missing verb.

4 Experiments and Results

4.1 Baseline SMT

We used Joshua 4.0 as our baseline system using default settings. Training data was extracted from a parallel corpus based on the NSPEC corpus tested by (Mohaghegh & Sarrafzadeh, 2012). After some modification to remove inconsistencies in the translation output, the final corpus (names NPEC) consisted of almost 85,000 sentence pairs of 1.4 million words, originating mostly from bilingual news sites. There are a number of different domains covered in this corpus, but the majority of the texts were in literature, science and conversation. The language model used in the tests was extracted from IRNA[5] website, covering news stories, and comprised over 66 million words.

4.2 Test Data Set

Our evaluation is based on eight test sets extracted from certain bilingual websites. Randomly selected, test sentences cover different domains such as art, medicine, economics and news. The direction of translation is English-Persian. In the evaluation process, the Persian side of the test sets was used as the translation reference to score the output quality of both the baseline system and the final post-APE output. The size of the test data varies from one paragraph of text (more than 100 words) to a complete page or more (up to 600 words). The number of sentences in both sides is equal. The total number of test sentences is 153. The reason the number of test sentences was less than what would normally be preferred is that finding perfectly correct human translations for sentences for scoring purposes covering a number of domains is a very difficult task and manual evaluation by annotators would be much more labor-intensive.

4.3 Automatic Evaluation

We used both BLEU and NIST to evaluate the effect of APE system on translation quality. The results of translation before and after APE are shown in Table 1.

As Figures 2 and 3 also demonstrate, the results generally show increases in both metrics. The greatest increase in BLEU score due to the APE was achieved in test set #3, with an increase of about 0.15 BLEU, while the greatest NIST score increase was in test set #1, with a 0.16 increase.

However, in certain test sets the scoring metrics report a decrease in output quality, the worst BLEU score being at a difference of -0.0151, and the worst NIST at -0.27. The main reason behind weakened results is lack of training data for the Transliterator module, as it scripted some proper names and terms incorrectly in Persian. The large difference between the BLEU scores of data sets is due to each data set genre and the type of training data set. The quality of statistical translation (in terms of BLEU metric score) affects the APE module directly. The test set is in the news story domain, the same domain as the parallel corpus

[4] Non-Verbal Element: Many Persian verbs are compound verbs. They consist of two parts; one verbal and one non-verbal element.

[5] http://www.irna.ir/ENIndex.htm

Input	Size(words)		Before APE		After APE		BLEU Difference	NIST Difference
	En	Fa	BLEU	NIST	BLEU	NIST		
#1	163	158	0.6523	6.5740	0.6770	6.7349	0.0247	0.1609
#2	218	222	0.2232	1.0870	0.2187	1.0935	-0.0045	0.0065
#3	371	403	0.5914	6.1083	0.7388	6.1089	0.1474	0.0006
#4	362	337	0.1365	0.7962	0.1214	0.7064	-0.0151	-0.0898
#5	101	115	0.7925	5.7332	0.8716	5.4624	0.0791	-0.2708
#6	354	386	0.2738	1.8922	0.2779	1.9196	0.0041	0.0274
#7	555	653	0.2945	2.0457	0.2951	2.0333	0.0006	-0.0124
#8	259	297	0.4048	2.3940	0.4089	2.4052	0.0041	0.0112

Table 1. Scores of APE based on SMT Joshua version 4.0

used. In test set #4, in the religious genre, the decrease in both BLEU and NIST is attributed to a lack of data in this genre.

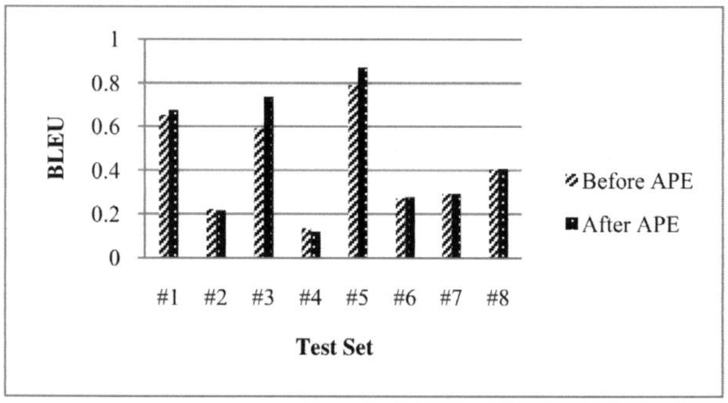

Figure 2. Difference of BLEU score after applying APE on eight test sets

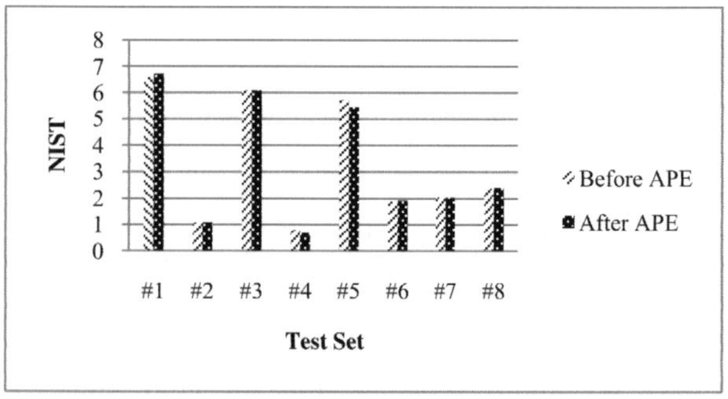

Figure 3. Difference of NIST score after applying APE

4.4 Manual Evaluation

As suggested by (Marecek et al., 2011), grammatical correctness of sentences cannot be measured appropriately with BLEU metrics. Because of this, we evaluated the output manually. The same test sets in automatic evaluation containing 153 sentences are evaluated here. We assigned the APE output of test sentences to two separate annotators, instructing them to rank the APE output sentences based on whether the output showed improvement, decrease, or no change in fluency compared to the original SMT output. Table 2 summarizes the results of this manual evaluation.

Annotator/ Rank	**Improved**	**No Change**	Weakened
Annotator 1	47	95	11
Annotator 2	43	99	11

Table 2. Manual evaluation scores for 153 test sentences

Both annotators, who completed the evaluation without discussing or consulting with each other, had very similar judgment of the APE system's output. The results show that the APE system has been successful in improving the quality of the baseline SMT system output by 29.4%. The current developed rules for the APE system are effective for about 37% of the SMT translated sentences.

We also identified both annotator agreements on ranked sentences. Based on their agreement, the quality improvement from the APE system is 25% and weakened by 3%. The comparison of the average percent of manual scores is shown in Figure 4.

5 Conclusion and Future Work

We presented an uncommon automatic post-

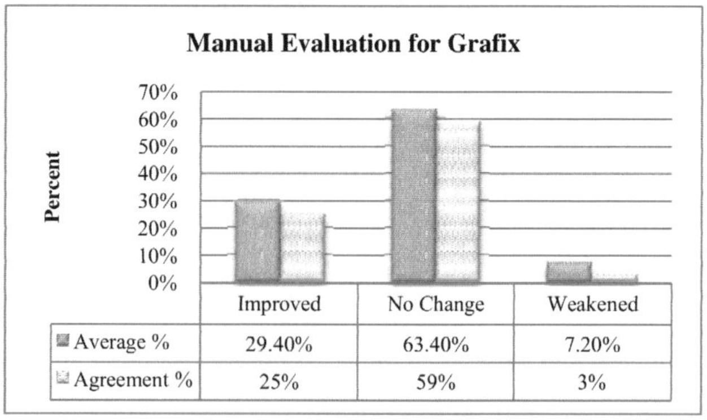

Figure 4. Manual evaluation of 153 test sentences

editing model for English-Persian statistical machine translation developed using a rule-based approach in different levels of transformation. The automatic evaluation results in terms of BLEU metric show that 75% of the test sets have been improved as far as the quality of the translation is concerned after post-editing. Although is affected by the quality of SMT system output, our APE approach is shown to be able to improve the SMT output up to 0.15 BLEU. On the other hand we faced some decrease in quality of translation by applying the system. We found that these results came from the lexical transformer level. We believe that this is due to OOV words remaining in the original script, and that the application of OOVRemover and Transliterator only produced a new unknown (incorrect) word as the original word equivalent. This phenomenon has decreased the BLEU score in one case by up to -0.015 BLEU.

Our results in terms of NIST and BLEU show that automatic evaluation could not reveal the quality of grammatical changes appropriately. However, manual evaluation scores show that a rule-based approach for an APE system is useful for improving at least 25% of the translation with a loss of at most 7%. To increase the improvement and decrease the loss of accuracy, we intend to enrich the bilingual dictionary used in OOVRemover as well as training data for Transliterator. Extending the rules in both shallow and deep levels is another task we plan to focus on. We also intend to investigate the use of an automatic rule induction module using text mining or similar approaches.

References

Ahsan, A., Kolachina, P., Kolachina, S., Sharma, D. M., & Sangal, R. (2010). Coupling statistical machine translation with rule-based transfer and generation. *In Proceedings of the 9th Conference of the Association for Machine Translation in the Americas*. Denver, Colorado.

Allen, J., & Hogan, C. (2000). Toward the Development of a Post-editing Module for Raw Machine Translation Output: A Controlled Language Perspective. *Third International Controlled Language Applications Workshop (CLAW-00)* (pp. 62-71).

Ambati, V. (2008). Dependency Structure Trees in Syntax Based Machine Translation. In Advanced MT Seminar Course Report.

Buchholz, S., & Marsi, E. (2006). CoNLL-X shared task on multilingual dependency parsing. *In Proceedings of the Tenth Conference on Computational Natural Language Learning* (pp. 149-164). New York City, USA: Association for Computational Linguistics.

Callison-Burch, C., Koehn, P., Monz, C., & Zaidan, O. F. (2011). *Findings of the 2011 workshop on statistical machine translation.*

Chiang, D. (2005). A hierarchical phrase-based model for statistical machine translation *In Proceedings of the 43rd Annual Meeting on Association for Computational Linguistics* (pp. 263-270). University of Michigan, USA.: Association for Computational Linguistics.

Chiang, D. (2007). Hierarchical phrase-based translation. *Computational Linguistics, 33*(2), 201-228.

Crystal, D. (2004). The Cambridge Encyclopedia of English Language: Ernst Klett Sprachen.

Ding, Y., & Palmer, M. (2005). Machine translation using probabilistic synchronous dependency insertion grammars *In Proceedings of the 43rd Annual Meeting on Association for Computational Linguistics* (pp. 541-548). Ann Arbor, USA: Association for Computational Linguistics.

Hudson, R. A. (1984). Word grammar: Blackwell Oxford.

Isabelle, P., Goutte, C., & Simard, M. (2007). Domain adaptation of MT systems through automatic post-editing *In Proceedings of Machine Translation Summit XI* (pp. 255-261). Phuket, Thailand.

Kübler, S., McDonald, R., & Nivre, J. (2009). Dependency parsing *Synthesis Lectures on Human Language Technologies* (Vol. 1, pp. 1-127).

Lagarda, A. L., Alabau, V., Casacuberta, F., Silva, R., & Diaz-de-Liano, E. (2009). Statistical post-editing of a rule-based machine translation system. *Proceedings of Human Language Technologies: The 2009 Annual Conference of the North American Chapter of the Association for Computational Linguistics, Companion Volume: Short Papers* (pp. 217-220). Boulder, Colorado: Association for Computational Linguistics.

Li, Z., Callison-Burch, C., Khudanpur, S., & Thornton, W. (2009). Decoding in Joshua. *Prague Bulletin of Mathematical Linguistics, 91*, 47-56.

Marecek, D., Rosa, R., & Bojar, O. (2011). Two-step translation with grammatical post-processing. *In Proceedings of the Sixth Workshop on Statistical Machine Translation* (pp. 426-432). Stroudsburg, PA,USA: Association for Computational Linguistics.

McDonald, R., Pereira, F., Ribarov, K., & Hajic, J. (2005). Non-projective dependency parsing using spanning tree algorithms. *In Proceedings of the conference on Human Language Technology and Empirical Methods in Natural Language Processing* (pp. 523-530). Vancouver, B.C., Canada: Association for Computational Linguistics.

Mohaghegh, M., & Sarrafzadeh, A. (2012). *A hierarchical phrase-based model for English-Persian statistical machine translation.*

Mohaghegh, M., Sarrafzadeh, A., & Moir, T. (2011). *Improving Persian-English Statistical Machine Translation: Experiments in Domain Adaptation.*

Pilevar, A. H. (2011). USING STATISTICAL POST-EDITING TO IMPROVE THE OUTPUT OF RULE-BASED MACHINE TRANSLATION SYSTEM. *Training, 330*, 330,000.

Raja, F., Amiri, H., Tasharofi, S., Sarmadi, M., Hojjat, H., & Oroumchian, F. (2007). Evaluation of part of speech tagging on Persian text. *University of Wollongong in Dubai-Papers*, 8.

Rasooli, M. S., Moloodi, A., Kouhestani, M., & Minaei-Bidgoli, B. (2011). A syntactic valency lexicon for Persian verbs: The first steps towards Persian dependency treebank. *In Proceedings of 5th Language & Technology Conference (LTC): Human Language Technologies as a Challenge for Computer Science and Linguistics* (pp. 227-231).

Rosa, R., Marecek, D., & Duˇsek, O. (2012). DEPFIX: A System for Automatic Correction of Czech MT Outputs. *In Proceedings of the Seventh Workshop on Statistical Machine Translation,* . Montreal, Canada: Association for Computational Linguistics.

Simard, M., Goutte, C., & Isabelle, P. (2007). Statistical phrase-based post-editing *In Human LanguageTechnologies 2007: The Conference of the North American Chapter of the Association for Computational Linguistics; Proceedings of the Main Conference* (pp. 508-515). Rochester, USA.

Weese, J., Ganitkevitch, J., Callison-Burch, C., Post, M., & Lopez, A. (2011). *Joshua 3.0: Syntax-based machine translation with the thrax grammar extractor.*

Xuan, H., Li, W., & Tang, G. (2011). An Advanced Review of Hybrid Machine Translation (HMT). *Procedia Engineering, 29*, 3017-3022.

Zollmann, A., & Venugopal, A. (2006). Syntax augmented machine translation via chart parsing. *In Proceedings of the Workshop on Statistical Machine Translation* (pp. 138-141). New York City, USA: Association for Computational Linguistics.

Statistical Stemming for Kannada

Suma Bhat
Beckman Institute for Advanced Science and Technology,
University of Illinois,
Urbana-Champaign, IL 61801, USA
spbhat2@illinois.edu

Abstract

Stemming is a process that groups morphologically related words into the same class and is widely used in information retrieval for improving recall rate. Here we study a set of statistical stemmers for Kannada, a resource-poor language with highly inflectional and agglutinative morphology. We compare stemming using simple truncation, clustering and an unsupervised morpheme segmentation algorithm on a sample from a text collection.

We observe that a distance measure that rewards longest prefix matches is the best performing clustering-based stemmer. However, using a reasonably performing unsupervised morpheme segmentation seems to outperform the other stemming schemes considered.

1 Introduction

With the ongoing quest for developing language processing techniques and tools for under-resourced languages there is an emerging need to study various aspects of these languages. Kannada, with nearly 70 million speakers is one of the 40 most spoken languages in the world. It is one of the scheduled languages of India and the official and administrative language of the state of Karnataka in South India. Its rich literary heritage has endowed the language with an immense written resource and efforts are currently underway to bring them to web scales. However, available computational tools for Kannada are only in their incipient stages. Simultaneously, there is an ever increasing number of internet users who are creating online materials in Kannada. As more information becomes available it becomes imperative to develop language processing tools that help us organize, search and understand information in Kannada. One such task is that of information retrieval and the time is ripe for developing language processing tools for efficient information retrieval in Kannada.

Stemming serves to conflate morphologically related word forms into a common form. The role of stemming in improving retrieval effectiveness, particularly for highly inflected languages and monolingual retrieval has been well documented in studies including (Larkey and Connell, 2003; Majumder et al., 2007; Dolamic and Savoy, 2010). In addition, the efficiency of IR systems owing to a decrease in size of the index term set (and a concomitant decrease in storage) is an added effect of stemming. Consequently, with the goal of developing a suitable stemmer for Kannada (a resource-poor language as far as current language processing resources are concerned), the focus of this study is statistical approaches to stemming in Kannada. We study stemming via three strategies. The first is truncation by a prefix of certain length, the second, a clustering approach using string distance measures and the third involves using the result of unsupervised morpheme segmentation. In this context the goals of the current study are the following.

1. To choose the most effective distance measure from among a set of string distance measures and determine a distance threshold that results in good stemming performance; and,

2. To compare the performance of the resulting clustering-based stemmer with traditional algorithms such as truncation and unsupervised morpheme segmentation.

For the purpose of this study, we evaluate the stemming performance without distinguishing between inflectional and derivational morphology.

The rest of this paper is organized as follows. In Section 2 a description in brief of prior research related to our study is presented. Section 3 deals with a description of the data used. The methodology used in the study is the content of Section 4. The experimental details are found in Section 5. Section 6 highlights the results and the related analysis occurs in Section 7. In Section 8 we present conclusions drawn from the study and outline some directions for further study.

2 Prior Work

As a recall enhancing technique in IR and efficient storage mechanism (since morphologically related word forms are conflated to the same stem), various stemming procedures have been studied for several languages. Stemming experiments and their effectiveness in IR have been carried out for English and other European languages (Goldsmith et al., 2000; Savoy, 2006; Fautsch and Savoy, 2009; Korenius et al., 2004; Majumder et al., 2008) and for a few Indian languages (Majumder et al., 2007; Dolamic and Savoy, 2010). There is empirical evidence that a stemming procedure improves retrieval effectiveness when applied to European languages including French, Portuguese, German and Hungarian (Savoy, 2006). For processing agglomerative languages such as Turkish and Finnish, stemming effectiveness has been studied (Ekmekçioglu and Willett, 2000; Sever and Bitirim, 2003; Korenius et al., 2004). Further, indexing and search strategies have been found to perform significantly better with the application of the various stemming strategies (compared to an indexing scheme without a stemmer), for Hindi, Bengali and Marathi (Dolamic and Savoy, 2010; Majumder et al., 2007). Retrieval experiments on English, French, Bengali, Hindi and Marathi datasets show that a statistical stemming approach via clustering is effective for languages that are primarily suffixing in nature (Majumder et al., 2007; Dolamic and Savoy, 2010; Ekmekçioglu and Willett, 2000; Sever and Bitirim, 2003).

As an effective bootstrapping approach to stemming, statistical methods have been explored for several languages. The popular stemming algorithms for English are based on language-specific rules explored in (Lovins, 1968) and (Porter, 1980), whereas for several other languages statistical stemming has been considered. The statistical stemmer studied in (Majumder et al., 2007; Šnajder and Bašic, 2009) is a cluster-based suffix stripping algorithm, whereas a probabilistic suffix stripping algorithm is explored in (Di Nunzio et al., 2004). In (Ekmekçioglu and Willett, 2000) a rule-based morphological analysis stemmer is used for Turkish.

Studies on developing morphological analyzers (mostly rule-based) for Kannada are available (Antony et al., 2010; Veerappan et al., 2011; Shastri, 2011; Murthy, 1999), but there have been no reports of evaluations of their propositions in terms of stemming effectiveness. In (Bhat, 2012), a preliminary study of unsupervised algorithms for morpheme segmentation in Kannada is available which observed that a statistical morpheme segmentation algorithm such as (Dasgupta and Ng, 2006) shows a reasonable performance for morpheme segmentation in Kannada. Taking the results of prior studies further, the current study is cast in the knowledge-base gained and compares stemming using a clustering-based approach with stemming using simple truncation and that using an unsupervised morpheme segmentation algorithm. The favorable results of prior studies with languages that are primarily suffixing in nature and those of the agglutinative type, prompts us to consider their stemming approaches for Kannada.

2.1 Challenges to Morphological Analysis in Kannada

Kannada is one of the four major literary languages of the Dravidian family. Kannada is mainly an agglutinating language of the strongly suffixing type (Dryer and Haspelmath, 2011; Sridhar, 1990). Words contain a basic root, with one or more suffixes being combined with this root in order to extend its meaning or to create other classes of words. Agglutination can result in long words that can contain as much semantic information as a whole English phrase, clause or sentence. An example of this characteristic is provided by the word, *sadupayOgapaDisikoLLabahudu* 'could avail the benefits'. Nouns are marked for number and case and verbs are marked, in most cases, for agreement with the subject in number, gender and person (like other nouns, geographical, product and even proper names are marked with case endings making the use of a dictionary impractical). This makes Kannada a relatively free word order language. Morphologically rich languages such as Kannada, are characterized by a large number of morphemes in a single word, where morpheme boundaries are difficult to detect because they are fused together. In addition, rampant morphophonemic processes (sandhi), productive compounding and agglutinating morphology of inflectional and derivational suffixes (the latter mostly with words of Sanskrit origin naturalized into Kannada) drive the prolific word formation processes of the language (Sridhar, 1990).

3 Data

Corpus: For the purpose of experimentation we use the Kannada portion of the EMILLE corpus (Baker et al., 2002). In order to avoid words with typographical errors we restrict the sample to those word types occurring at least two times. Here, instead of resorting to clustering the lexicon from the given collection, we reduce the computational cost of the experiment by focusing on a subset of the lexicon. Thus, our experimental data set has 10020 words which are chosen so as to include the most morphologically productive words (manually chosen from the lexicon). We consider a suitable Roman transliteration of the Kannada unicode characters for computational ease.

Gold set: For evaluating the stemmers, we manually group the related forms of words in the sample into equivalence classes. In preparing the classes we do not distinguish between inflectionally and derivationally related forms. Thus, morphologically and semantically related words occur in the same group (for instance, compound forms semantically related to the root word occur in the same class). Moreover, in the case of polysemy, it suffices if some of their senses are related (note that semantic relations between members of such groups are less clear without the context). In such cases, the sense was arbitrarily chosen. It is worth pointing out that the groups here leave out compound words where the anchoring word occurs in the non-first position (a feature not intrinsic to Kannada, but derived from Sanskrit - e.g. *mahAraja* "great king" is derived from *raja* "king"). Our resulting gold set of equivalence classes consists of 667 such groups. Table 1 shows an excerpt from the sample in which 34 word forms occur in the same group.

4 Method

We perform a clustering-based approach to discover equivalence classes of root words and their morphological variants. Using a set of string distance measures a subset of a given text collection in Kannada is clustered to identify these equivalence classes. The proposed approach is compared with simple truncation based stemming and that based on unsupervised morpheme segmentation.

4.1 String Distance Measures

We consider the set of string distance measures proposed in (Majumder et al., 2007) for clustering a set of words. The distance measures assign a real value (distance) to a pair of strings, with the distance being indicative of the similarity between the two strings - a smaller value means higher similarity between the strings. Accordingly, we define the distance between two identical strings to be 0. For two strings X and Y, (if X and Y are of unequal length, we pad the shorter string with null characters to make the string lengths equal) let the length of the strings be $n + 1$. Let m denote the position of the first mismatch between X and Y. The distance measures are given by,

$$D_2(X, Y) = \frac{1}{m} \sum_{i=m}^{n} \frac{1}{2^{i-m}},$$

$$D_3(X, Y) = \frac{n - m + 1}{m} \sum_{i=m}^{n} \frac{1}{2^{i-m}},$$

$$D_4(X, Y) = \frac{n - m + 1}{n + 1} \sum_{i=m}^{n} \frac{1}{2^{i-m}}.$$

Intuitively, measure D_2 rewards long matching prefixes, D_4 penalizes long non-matching suffixes and D_3 does both. Motivated by the the effectiveness of the statistical stemmer (using the three measures) for the Indian languages - Hindi, Marathi and Bengali - as in (Majumder et al., 2007; Dolamic and Savoy, 2010), we use the same measures to study stemming for Kannada which is of the strongly suffixing type.

4.2 Clustering

We cluster the word forms using a hierarchical agglomerative algorithm as studied in (Majumder et al., 2007). The algorithm starts by assigning word forms to singleton clusters and proceeds by merging at each level the two least distant clusters until a single cluster remains. At each merging stage, the distance between two clusters is computed as one of the maximum, minimum, or average distance between the elements of the two

vidyArthi, vidyArthigU ,vidyArthigaLU , vidyArthigaLa, vidyArthigaLalli, vidyArthigaLalliruva, vidyArthigaLannU
vidyArthigaLannu, vidyArthigaLeMdare,vidyArthigaLiMda, vidyArthigaLigAgi, vidyArthigaLigU, vidyArthigaLige, vidyArthigaLigiMta
vidyArthigaLirabEku, vidyArthigaLoMdige, vidyArthigaLu, vidyArthige, vidyArthiniyara, vidyArthinilaya, vidyArthinilayada
vidyArthinilayadalli, vidyArthinilayagaLu, vidyArthinilayakke, vidyArthiyAgi, vidyArthiyAgiddAga, vidyArthiyAgidda, vidyArthiyAgiddaru
vidyArthiyAgidde, vidyArthiyU, vidyArthiya, vidyArthiyannu, vidyArthiyobbana, vidyArthiyu

Table 1: An example of a word group with words derived from *vidyArthi* "student"

clusters, referred to as complete-linkage, single-linkage, and average-linkage algorithm, respectively. Complete-linkage results in small and compact clusters, single-linkage results in long and branched clusters, whereas the result of average linkage is somewhere in between (in contrast to single linkage, each element needs to be relatively similar to all members of the other cluster, rather than to just one). For our experiment, we use average-linkage clustering. The resulting hierarchical structure is only used to the extent that members along a branch (below a certain distance) belong to the same cluster.

The main drawback of hierarchical agglomerative clustering is its computational inefficiency. Because the number of word forms in our sample is of the order of thousands, we adopt the following complexity reducing technique before proceeding to the hierarchical clustering step. We carry out the clustering in two consecutive steps: a divisive step followed by an agglomerative step. The idea is to use the divisive step to partition the set of word forms into pre-clusters and then to perform agglomerative clustering on each of the pre-clusters separately. In order to facilitate the merging of morphologically related words in the agglomerative step, it is essential that the pre-clusters be sufficiently coarse grained. We first group the words into pre-clusters by truncating them to the first n characters, $n = 1, \ldots, 7$. For a given prefix length, this results in a set of pre-clusters. This step serves a two-fold purpose in this study; it not only reduces the computational complexity, but also serves as a baseline for comparing the stemming performance of the subsequent hierarchical clustering step.

4.3 Unsupervised Morpheme Segmentation Algorithm

We consider an extension of Keshava and Pitler's algorithm (Keshava and Pitler, 2006) for language-independent morpheme induction studied in (Dasgupta and Ng, 2006). This algorithm was chosen since it was the overall best performing morpheme segmentation algorithm as studied in (Bhat, 2012) with a favorable F-measure of 72%. The algorithm (hereafter abbreviated as *Morphind*) being unsupervised, accepts as input an untagged corpus as a list of words with their frequency occurrence in the corpus. The key idea for morpheme discovery used here is that the conditional probability of a letter given its context exhibits a sudden jump at a morpheme boundary. The algorithm proceeds by first creating a forward tree and a backward tree, which provide the basis for efficient calculation of transitional probabilities of a letter given its context. It is then followed by the affix acquisition step, during which a set of morphemes is identified from the corpus. The third step uses the morphemes identified to segment words.

4.4 Evaluation

Since the explicit benefit of stemming is seen in the realm of information retrieval (IR), in several prior studies, the performance of a stemming algorithm is traditionally evaluated by considering the effect on the performance of IR systems. Conducting such a task-specific evaluation makes it impossible to assess cases where the stemmer makes faulty conflations and/or cases of correct conflation. In order to enable such an analysis we use a task-independent evaluation first proposed by Paice (1996). In this method of stemmer evaluation, the actual understemming and overstemming errors committed are counted on a manually constructed word sample in which the words are grouped based on their morphological relatedness. The understemming index (UI) is computed as the proportion of pairs from the sample that are relegated to different groups by the stemmer even though they are related; the overstemming index (OI) is computed as the proportion of pairs that actually belong to different groups among those that are conflated to the same stem. As in (Šnajder and Bašic, 2009) we resort to measure the overall stemming effectiveness in terms of stemming quality (SQ), defined as the harmonic mean of 1-

UI and 1-OI.

5 Experiments

5.1 Stemming Algorithms

We use *Morphind* with its default parameters (which govern the size of the suffix list for segmentation) as in (Bhat, 2012). The algorithm excludes from its analysis words seen only once in the corpus. This has the obvious disadvantage that several morphological variants are lost from being considered for the analysis.

5.2 Clustering

The distance threshold during the agglomerative clustering procedure governs the stemming quality; a lower threshold corresponds to 'light' stemming and a higher threshold corresponds to a heavier stemming. In (Majumder et al., 2007), the optimum distance threshold in the hierarchical clustering stage was chosen based upon the number of clusters being generated. As in (Šnajder and Bašic, 2009), we choose the optimum threshold for hierarchical clustering by looking at the stemming quality obtained by stemming the words in the gold set. The optimum threshold is chosen to be that which maximizes the stemming quality.

6 Results

Experiments were conducted using the sample of 10020 words and evaluated against the manually created equivalence classes of 667 groups.

6.1 Pre-clustering

Length	Total	Largest	UI	OI	SQ
1	26	1106	0.00	0.87	0.23
2	125	406	0.00	0.62	0.55
3	258	382	0.00	0.37	0.77
4	432	280	0.14	0.27	0.79
5	949	234	0.53	0.21	0.59
6	1840	108	0.73	0.03	0.42
7	2976	66	0.85	0.01	0.26

Table 2: Total number of clusters, size of the largest cluster, understemming (UI), overstemming (OI) indices and stemming quality (SQ) in the pre-clustering stage with different prefix lengths

The divisive step of clustering, with word forms truncated to the first n letters, $n = 1, \dots, 7$, results in a set of clusters whose details are tabulated in Table 2. For each partition, we indicate the number of clusters, the size of the largest cluster, the understemming and overstemming indices and the stemming quality. The understemming index reflects the errors made by truncation (assigning morphologically related word forms to distinct pre-clusters by truncating to a prefix of given length). The problem of pre-clustering with a common fixed-length prefix is that, in order to obtain pre-clusters of manageable sizes, the prefix length must be high. This splits apart many morphologically related groups, as indicated by the increasing understemming values as we move down the column.

From Table 2, we notice that SQ peaks at a pre-clustering level of length 4. However, we also observe that the pre-clusters with a common prefix of length 3 have a lower understemming index. With the primary goal of keeping a low UI, and knowing that once split at the pre-clustering level, related words cannot be merged during the subsequent clustering stages, we choose pre-clusters with a common prefix of length 3 for subsequent agglomerative clustering. For hierarchical clustering, we use the distance measures D_2, D_3 and D_4 as defined in Section 4.1.

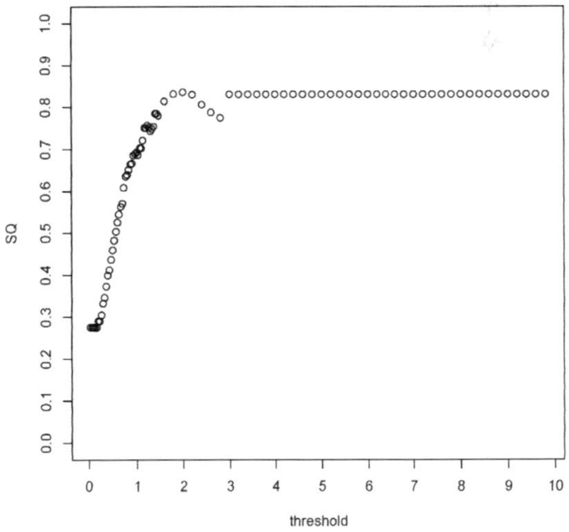

Figure 1: Plot of the stemming quality of clustering using the distance measure D_2 as a function of the distance threshold

In Figure 1, SQ of measure D_2 as a function of the threshold is shown. Measure D_2 achieves the optimal stemming quality for a threshold of 2.0 and the maximum stemming quality is 83.46%.

Stemmer	t	UI%	OI%	SQ%
D_2	2.0	10.19	22.05	**83.46**
D_3	35.8	11.53	23.08	82.10
D_4	7.0	0.17	28.97	83.00
trunc(3)	-	0.25	36.69	77.20
Morphind	-	19.65	0.7	**88.82**

Table 3: Comparison of the optimal stemming performances of the approaches studied

Table 3 shows the optimal stemming quality of the string distance measures and the corresponding distance threshold values t. We note that clustering using measure D_2 yields the best performance for stemming by clustering. We notice that the optimum SQ, however, comes at the expense of a higher UI compared to the truncation scheme.

Next, comparing the stemming performance via clustering with that resulting from morpheme segmentation, we notice that the higher stemming quality (88.82%) in the latter case comes at the cost of a significantly higher UI.

The OI-UI plot on Figure 2 shows the stemming performance of the three distance measures. In particular, the OI-UI variation while varying the distance threshold is shown (since the distance thresholds were different for each measure, the corresponding information was omitted from the plot). As the value of the distance threshold increases, clusters are merged resulting in decreased UI and an increase in OI. The plot reveals that for the most part, the three measures perform better than simple truncation.

7 Discussion

An evaluation of the stemming performance crucially depends on the manually created groups of morphologically related word forms. Given that the grouping process was done by subjective human judgement rather than an objective criterion, variations in grouping are highly likely. For instance, semantic relatedness of words is different depending on the context and has varied granularity. To cite an example, consider the word group shown in Table 1. The group consists of words derived from *vidyArthi* "student". While *vidyArthigaLu* "students (nominative plural)" is related to *vidyArthi* by inflectional morphology, *vidyArthini* "female student" is also related and so is *vidyArthinilaya* " student residence" or *vidyArthivEtana* "financial aid (scholarship)". Depending on the topic being discussed, "student residence" and "scholarship" may be grouped together with "student" or not. We would like to remind the fact that words were grouped based only on their surface form with no additional information (such as context). It is important to also note here that in order to facilitate a clustering process, only words related by a suffixing process were grouped together which means that the manual grouping process has an inherent UI. As a result, words such as *BASe* "language" and *ADuBASe* "vernacular (common language)" were relegated to different groups.

With the choice of an appropriate distance threshold (for a description see Section 5.2), the SQ by clustering using measure D_2 can exceed 80%. Thus, clustering using string distance measures seems to be a favorable statistical stemming approach compared to simple truncation, which (on the same sample) reaches to SQ = 77.20%. The agreeable stemming quality of the truncation method suggests that a simplistic statistical stemmer, of taking fixed length substrings of words as stems, may in itself, result in an increased performance for IR.

The ease of implementation of the clustering procedure could be considered as an advantage over *Morphind*, which requires an informed setting of its parameters (language-dependent) for optimum segmentation performance. A more conclusive comparison of the two methods will have to be done in a task-specific setting such as that of IR evaluation.

Let us now take a look at an instance of the clustering procedure. We begin with the pre-cluster 'vid' (which included the group of words in Table 1) which was later clustered hierarchically. At the optimum threshold of t = 2.0, with the distance measure D_2, the group consisting of the morphological variants of *vidyArthi* was clustered along with the words found in Table 5. Here we notice that the words are broadly related, but certainly do not belong to the same group, indicating the source of understemming error.

We next look at the stemming (via morphological segmentation) of the set of words in the same Table 1 and notice that they have been divided into five groups in addition to the obvious first group, **vidyArthi**: there is **vidyArthiniyara**,

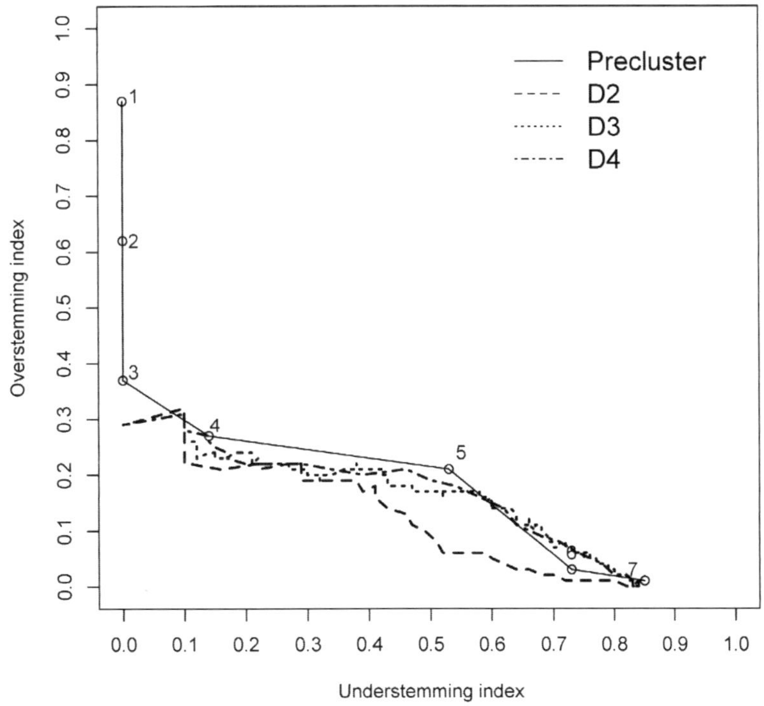

Figure 2: UI-OI plots of the hierarchical clustering with the distance measures compared with that in the pre-clustering with different prefix lengths

Method	No. of stems	Compression (%)
Gold set	666	93.00
Clustering(D2)	227	97.61
Truncation(3)	258	97.29
Morphind	1946	79.57

Table 4: Compression rates compared

vidyArthigaL, **vidyArthiyAgidde**, **vidyArthiyobbana** and **vidyArthinilaya**. The resulting overstemming error can be attributed to the inability of the morpheme segmentation algorithm to handle word forms such as *vidyArthinilaya* and *vidyArthiyAgidde* (compounding) and *vidyArthiyobbana* (external sandhi).

Another perspective of the stemming performance can be seen in Table 4. Here we list the compression rates in terms of the number of reduced words in the dictionary after stemming. The rather high compression ratio in the manually created grouping can be explained by noticing that the words comprise a subsample of the word types occurring in the collection chosen from among the most productive words occurring in the corpus. (True compression rates of the lexicon are expected to be lower than what is noted here, but certainly higher than that of English since the morphology is more complex than that of English.) Notice how the morpheme segmentation algorithm results in the creation of about three times as many groups as needed. This explains the corresponding high UI and low OI in Table 3

In the current study, the manually created equivalence classes did not distinguish between inflectional and derivational forms. If such a grouping were to be available, the distance threshold could have been tuned to isolate inflectionally related forms from derivationally related forms.

We are then interested to see how morphological variants are ranked based on their distance

vidyA2ara,vidyA2arara,vidyA2ikAri,vidyAByAsa,vidyAByAsada,vidyAByAsadalli,vidyAByAsakkAgi, vidyAByAsakke,vidyAByAsavannu,vidyAbud2i,vidyAbud2ivaMtaru,vidyAdAna,vidyAlayada,vidyAlayagaLalli, vidyAmaMtrigaLa,vidyAni2i,vidyAnilayada,vidyApariNitaru,vidyArthivEtana,vidyArthivEtanavannu,vidyAraNya, vidyAraNyara,vidyArhate,vidyArjaneyalli,vidyAsaMs4egaLalli,vidyAtajxara,vidyAvaMta,vidyAvaMtanAgalu, vidyAvaMtanU,vidyAvaMtarAdarU,vidyAvaMtarAgi,vidyAvaMtarU,vidyAvaMtara,vidyAvaMtaralli,vidyAvaMtarannAgi, vidyAvaMtarannu,vidyAvaMtarige,vidyAvaMtaru,vidye,vidyegU,vidyegaLa,vidyegaLannu, vidyeyAgide,vidyeya,vidyeyalli,vidyeyannU,vidyeyannu,vidyeyu

Table 5: The set of words clustered along with words derived from *vidyArthi* "student"

from the lemma (the dictionary form of the root). It would be convenient to have a distance measure that helps us distinguish between inflectional forms and derivational forms of a lemma. Towards this, we again consider the lemma *vidyArthi* "student" and its morphologically related forms in Table 1. We consider the distance between the lemma and the other forms using the measures D_2, D_3 and D_4 and rank order them with increasing order of distance (words with tied distances are grouped together and only the top-10 words are listed).

D2 = {**vidyArthi**, {**vidyArthigU**, **vidyArthige**, **vidyArthiyU**, **vidyArthiya**, **vidyArthiyu**}, {**vidyArthigaLU**, **vidyArthigaLa**, **vidyArthigaLu**, vidyArthiyAgi}, **vidyArthigaLalli** }

D3 = {**vidyArthi**, {**vidyArthigU**, **vidyArthige**, **vidyArthiyU**, **vidyArthiya**, **vidyArthiyu**}, {**vidyArthigaLU**, **vidyArthigaLa**, **vidyArthigaLu**, vidyArthiyAgi}, **vidyArthiyannu**}

D4 = {**vidyArthi**, {**vidyArthigU**, **vidyArthige**, **vidyArthiyU**, **vidyArthiya**, **vidyArthiyu**}, {**vidyArthigaLU**, **vidyArthigaLa**, **vidyArthigaLu**, vidyArthiyAgi}, **vidyArthiyannu**}

Here we observe that inflectionally related forms (in bold) are ranked higher than derivationally related forms. It is also worth pointing out that the stemming procedures considered here work by targeting the primarily suffixing processes of Kannada. As a result of this, forms related resulting via the umlauting process (such as *shikSaNa* becoming *shykSaNika* as a denominal adjective) are not conflated.

The stemming performance of *Morphind* is critically dependent upon the accuracy of the morpheme segmentation process. In (Bhat, 2012) an F-measure of 72% was reported. Upon closer inspection, we notice that several assumptions in the algorithm are specific to English, resulting in a low recall for Kannada, whose morphology is more complex than that of English. In particular, the assumptions that - all stems are valid words in the lexicon, affixes occur at the beginning or end of words only and affixation does not change stems - are clearly violated in Kannada. Moreover, as noted in (Bhat, 2012), morpheme segmentation is better for nouns than for verbs. An intuitive explanation here is that the noun inflectional process is seen more often than the verb variants.

8 Conclusions and Future Work

The results of the above experiment suggest that, for Kannada, the stemming performance of a truncation-based algorithm can be improved by subsequent clustering of the generated groups. Moreover a string distance measure, such as D_2, that rewards long matching prefixes emerges as an effective distance measure for clustering morphologically related words. Overall, comparing statistical stemmers, an unsupervised morpheme segmentation approach (such as *Morphind*) to stemming works better than a clustering-based approach in the case of Kannada.

We are well aware that a rule-based linguistic stemmer will perform better than a non-linguistic statistical stemmer. However, this exercise serves as a bootstrapping mechanism of the stemming process for Kannada. Looking ahead, the performance of an aggressive stemmer that not only removes inflectional suffixes but also removes derivational suffixes via a set of rules would be of interest.

This work does not account for possible word ambiguities since each word is taken as an isolated entity, and is grouped according to its typical connotation. As noted in (Paice, 1996), it would certainly be of interest to allow different senses of a word to be assigned to different groups, using information about the meaning of each specific word taken in its context.

Finally and most importantly, we plan to study stemming for Kannada in a task-specific setting such as that of IR evaluation as has been done in several related studies with other languages.

References

P. J. Antony, M.A. Kumar, and K. P. Soman. 2010. Paradigm based morphological analyzer for kannada language using machine learning approach. *International Journal on Advances in Computational Sciences and Technology ISSN*, pages 0973–6107.

Paul Baker, Andrew Hardie, Tony McEnery, Hamish Cunningham, and Robert Gaizauskas. 2002. Emille, a 67-million word corpus of indic languages: Data collection, mark-up and harmonisation. In *Proceedings of Language Resources and Evaluation Conference (LREC)*.

Suma Bhat. 2012. Morpheme segmentation for kannada standing on the shoulder of giants. In *Proceedings of the WSANLP*, pages 411–415.

Sajib Dasgupta and Vincent Ng. 2006. Unsupervised morphological parsing of bengali. *Language Resources and Evaluation*, 40(3):311–330.

Giorgio Di Nunzio, Nicola Ferro, Massimo Melucci, and Nicola Orio. 2004. Experiments to evaluate probabilistic models for automatic stemmer generation and query word translation. In *Comparative evaluation of multilingual information access systems*, pages 220–235. Springer.

Ljiljana Dolamic and Jacques Savoy. 2010. Comparative study of indexing and search strategies for the hindi, marathi, and bengali languages. *ACM Transactions on Asian Language Information Processing*, 9(3):1–24.

Matthew S. Dryer and Martin Haspelmath, editors. 2011. *The World Atlas of Language Structures Online*. Max Planck Digital Library, Munich, 2011 edition.

F Cuna Ekmekçioglu and Peter Willett. 2000. Effectiveness of stemming for turkish text retrieval. *PROGRAM-LONDON-ASLIB*, 34(2):195–200.

Claire Fautsch and Jacques Savoy. 2009. Algorithmic stemmers or morphological analysis? an evaluation. *Journal of the American Society for Information Science and Technology*, 60:16161624.

John Goldsmith, Derrick Higgins, and Svetlana Soglasnova. 2000. Automatic language-specific stemming in information retrieval. In *Proceedings of the Workshop on Cross-Language Evaluation Forum (CLEF)*, pages 273–284.

Samarth Keshava and Emily Pitler. 2006. A simpler, intuitive approach to morpheme induction. In *Proceedings of 2nd Pascal Challenges Workshop*, pages 31–35.

Tuomo Korenius, Jorma Laurikkala, Kalervo Järvelin, and Martti Juhola. 2004. Stemming and lemmatization in the clustering of finnish text documents. In *Proceedings of the thirteenth ACM international conference on Information and knowledge management*, CIKM '04, pages 625–633.

Leah S. Larkey and Margaret E. Connell. 2003. Structured queries, language modeling, and relevance modeling in cross-language information retrieval. In *Information Processing and Management Special Issue on Cross Language Information Retrieval*.

Julie Lovins. 1968. *Development of a stemming algorithm*. MIT Information Processing Group, Electronic Systems Laboratory.

Prasenjit Majumder, Mandar Mitra, Swapan Parui, Gobinda Kole, Pabitra Mitra, and Kalyankumar Datta. 2007. Yass: Yet another suffix stripper. *ACM transactions on information systems (TOIS)*, 25(4):18.

Prasenjit Majumder, Mandar Mitra, and Dipasree Pal. 2008. Bulgarian, hungarian and czech stemming using yass. In *Advances in Multilingual and Multimodal Information Retrieval*, pages 49–56. Springer.

Kavi Narayana Murthy. 1999. A network and process model for morphological analysis/generation. In *ICOSAL-2, the Second International Conference on South Asian Languages, Punjabi University, Patiala, India*.

Chris Paice. 1996. Method for evaluation of stemming algorithms based on error counting. *Journal of the American Society for Information Science*, 47(8):632–649.

Martin Porter. 1980. An algorithm for suffix stripping. *Program: electronic library and information systems*, 14(3):130–137.

Jacques Savoy. 2006. Light stemming approaches for the french, portuguese, german and hungarian languages. In *Proceedings of the 2006 ACM symposium on Applied computing*, SAC '06, pages 1031–1035.

Hayri Sever and Yıltan Bitirim. 2003. Findstem: analysis and evaluation of a turkish stemming algorithm. In *String Processing and Information Retrieval*, pages 238–251. Springer.

G. Shastri. 2011. Kannada morphological analyser and generator using trie. *IJCSNS*, 11(1):112.

Jan Šnajder and B Dalbelo Bašic. 2009. String distance-based stemming of the highly inflected croatian language. In *Proceedings of the International Conference RANLP-2009. Borovets, Bulgaria: Association for Computational Linguistics*, pages 411–415.

S.N. Sridhar. 1990. *Kannada*. Routledge.

Ramasamy Veerappan, P. J. Antony, S. Saravanan, and K. P Soman. 2011. A rule based kannada morphological analyzer and generator using finite state transducer. *International Journal of Computer Applications*, 27(10):45–52.

On Application of Conditional Random Field in Stemming of Bengali Natural Language Text

Sandipan Sarkar
IBM
sandipansarkar@gmail.com,
sandipan.sarkar@in.ibm.com

Sivaji Bandyopadhyay
Computer Science & Engineering Department,
Jadavpur University
sbandyopadhyay@cse.jdvu.ac.in,
sivaji_cse_ju@yahoo.com

Abstract

While stochastic route has been explored in solving the stemming problem, Conditional Random Field (CRF), a conditional probability based statistical model, has not been applied yet. We applied CRF to train a set of stemmers for Bengali natural language text. Care had been taken to design it language neutral so that same approach can be applied for other languages. The experiments yielded more than 86% accuracy.

1 Introduction

Applications of stochastic methods in solving the stemming problem is not new. Along the rule-based approaches, this approach had been used for since 1994. The obvious advantage of stochastic stemmers is their language neutrality. Unlike rule-based stemmers, statistical stemmers usually do not require any language specific knowledge. Thus this type of stemmers is generic and can be applied in any language.

Several supervised and unsupervised statistical methods were applied before to address the problem of stemming. The methods explored are Decision Tree (Schmid, 1994), HMM (Melucci and Orio, 2003), character n-gram (Mayfield and McNamee, 2003; Jordan et al., 2005), clustering (Garain and Datta, 2005; Majumder et al., 2007; Das and Bandyopadhyay, 2008) and many more novel techniques (Croft and Xu, 1995; Goldsmith et al., 2001; Bacchin et al., 2002; Gelbukh et al., 2004; Bacchin et al., 2005; Dasgupta and Ng, 2006; Hammarström, 2006; Bhamidipati and Pal, 2007; Pandey and Siddiqui, 2008; and Patel et al., 2010). However, we could not find any work where CRF has been used.

Conditional Random Field (Lafferty et al., 2001), a probabilistic model that helps in segmenting and labelling sequence data, is quite popular in various applications such as DNA sequencing (e.g. Culotta et al., 2005), image analysis (e.g. Wang et al., 2006) etc. In NLP field it is applied in word sequencing (e.g. Tseng et al., 2005) and POS tagging (e.g. Ekbal et al., 2007; Batuer and Sun 2009) extensively. However, we could not find any publication that applied CRF in stemming or lemmatisation task in Bengali or other language.

The problem of stemming can be seen as a labelling problem where a surface word needs to be labelled against its stem. Thus, our hypothesis was CRF can be a useful tool for stemming task. The objective of this work was to apply it in building stemmers and test its performance in Bengali natural language text.

2 Related Statistical Stemming Works

As part of his decision tree based POS tagger, Schmid (1994) discovered the co-relation between POS tags and inflections. With the aid of that he identified inflections while discovering POS from the surface words.

Croft and Xu (1995) proposed a statistical mechanism to improve the result of strong rule-based stemmers that suffered from overstemming problem. The proposed mechanism applied co-occurrence measure of two words. The idea was to build equivalence classes based on a standard strong stemmer and then to apply this measure among all the words in the class. The stemmer formed new classes by merging existing classes, if word pairs from those classes were found to have high co-occurrence.

Goldsmith et al. (2001) reported an automatic statistical stemmer that would analyse a corpus of any language and find out a set of suffix and stem possibilities. Such possibilities are assigned with empirical probabilities to determine the final stem. They developed a system, which was run on Italian, German and French corpora, and reported average precisions against interpolated recalls. However, in this publication, it was not clear how effective this stemmer was against no-stemming approach. Also they admitted that the system was at an early stage.

Next significant statistical stemmer was reported by Bacchin et al. (2002). The approach was to search the community of substrings, which were formed by interlinked prefixes and suffixes, for the best word splits. They compared the language independent statistical stemmer (SPLIT) with no-stemming approach and a Porter-like rule based stemmer (Porter, 1980). However, the reported results show that the SPLIT performed worse than the rule based stemmer and the performance improvement against no-stemming approach was 5% at best.

Mayfield and McNamee (2003) reported a language independent, character n-gram based approach to identify pseudo-stems. They compared the retrieval accuracy for pseudo-stems against unstemmed words and stems, which are obtained from Porter-like (Porter, 1980) stemmers, for Swedish, Dutch, Italian, French, Finnish, Spanish, English and German. For most of the cases, n-gram approach performed better than unstemmed words but underperformed for stemmed words.

Melucci and Orio (2003) reported another language independent statistical stemmer based on HMM. They ran a similar comparison exercise as reported in Mayfield and McNamee (2003) for German, English, Italian, French and Spanish. The relative performances were same as Mayfield and McNamee (2003).

Gelbukh et al. (2004) proposed a language-agnostic unsupervised statistical approach to discover simple stemming rules from a corpus. The approach was to identify the set of stems and inflections from a corpus, where every word of the corpus can be obtained by a concatenation of one member from stem and infection set respectively. Genetic algorithm was applied to keep the size of the stem and inflection sets minimal. Though Porter (1980) performed better than the proposed stemmer, it promised to be an acceptable approach for quick stemming tasks.

Bacchin et al. (2005) proposed a probabilistic mutual reinforcement enhancement on their previous work SPLIT (Bacchin et al., 2002). The hypothesis was that a valid stem-inflection pair would have more probability of occurrence than an invalid stem-inflection pair. They applied this model against an Italian corpus and compared that again with no-stemming approach and a Porter-like stemmer. The reported results showed that it performed better than no-stemming approach consistently. However, the comparison against Porter-like stemmer did not produce any consistent result.

Garain and Datta (2005) applied stemming in the context of Bengali image document retrieval system. The proposed approach was unsupervised clustering based on edit distance (Levenshtein, 1966) of two words. Once clusters are formed, stem of the cluster was identified as the longest substring common to all words in the cluster. The experiment was run on images of newspaper articles and achieved the stemming accuracy of 88.77%.

Jordan et al. (2005) proposed a character n-gram based unsupervised algorithm to find the morphemes from a corpus. The n-grams with highest probabilities of occurrence in a corpus became candidate morphemes. The test words were recursively split to compare with these candidate morphemes to identify the resultant morpheme composition of the word. It was run on English, Finnish and Turkish word lists. It was found that the IR retrieval performance improved in comparison to the no-stemming approach for English and Finnish, whereas, in case of Turkish, the performance was worse than no-stemming.

Dasgupta and Ng (2006) devised an unsupervised algorithm for any natural language text to induce the prefix, suffix and stems from an unannotated corpus without any prior morphotactics and morpho-phonological rules. The same algorithm was extended to detect composite suffixes. They reported an accuracy of 64.62% while the algorithm was run on Bengali text corpus.

Hammarström (2006) proposed an unsupervised algorithm for detecting suffixes and stems from any unannotated natural language corpus. The work suggested a ranking mechanism of potential suffixes using three measures – Frequency (how many times the suffix appeared), Curve Drop (whether the suffix is well segmented to the left), Random Adjustment (discriminates a random segment from a true suffix). It argued in favour of gold standard based accuracy measurement of stemmer rather than IR application based measurements. The algorithm was applied on Maori, English, Swedish and Kuku Yalanji and reported accuracy of more than 90% on a relatively small set of test data (200 words each). It compared the result with Porter stemmer (Porter, 1980) for English and the performance was found to be same.

Bhamidipati and Pal (2007) proposed a statistical approach to improve a given stemmer's (rule-based or statistical etc.) performance. The approach was to compute the distance between the multinomial distribution function of a word and that of a candidate stem. The words were sorted in descending order based on frequency. If the distance was small, then the word was put into the same class of the stem otherwise, the word was treated as a new stem class. When this approach was applied on top of Porter (1980) and Truncate(n) stemmers, it was observed that the stemming accuracies consistently improved.

Majumder et al. (2007) took a clustering approach to solve the stemming problem. The clusters were formed from the corpus based on the distance between two words. They argued that Levenshtein edit distance (Levenshtein, 1966) may not be appropriate for this purpose and thus proposed four different distance functions, which put weights on mismatches based on the character position in a decreasing manner. The nucleus of the cluster became the stem. For French this approach produced comparable results with respect to Porter-like (Porter, 1980) stemmer. For Bengali, in absence of a Porter-like stemmer, they showed that it significantly improved over no-stemming approach.

Pandey and Siddiqui (2008) proposed an unsupervised approach to identify the stem based on Goldsmith's model (Goldsmith et al., 2001). It calculated the probability of the split of the word based on all combinations of possible stem and inflection combination. It iterated the split probability based on a naïve Bayesian model. The split with maximum probability identified the stem. The accuracy for Hindi language was reported between 85% - 89%, which outperformed both Ramanathan and Rao (2003) (67% - 70%) and Larkey et al. (2003) (72%-78%).

Groenewald (2009) developed a stemmer for Setswana based on k-Nearest Neighbour algorithm using a relatively small training data set. The stemmer achieved 64.06% accuracy which was slightly better than that of Brits (2006), which was a rule based stemmer.

Like in Garain and Datta (2005), Das and Bandyopadhyay (2010) presented a clustering based stemming technique for Bengali. However, they applied this technique on text instead of image. The clusters were formed based on minimum edit distance (Levenshtein, 1966) based K-means clustering. The accuracy of the stemmer was reported to be 74.06%.

Patel et al. (2010) followed a hybrid approach to come up with a stemmer for Gujarati. The statistical unsupervised approach proposed by Goldsmith et al. (2001) was adopted, however, a hand-crafted suffix list was used to better understand the stem and inflection split probabilities. The accuracy of the stemmer was reported to be 67.86%, which received a 17% accuracy boost because of hand-crafted suffix.

3 Conditional Random Field

Among statistical models, Hidden Markov Model (HMM) is very popular for labelling and sequencing tasks. However, HMM is a generative model that defines a join probability distribution P(**X**, **Y**) where **X** and **Y** are random variables respectively ranging over the observation sequence **X** and state sequence **Y**. To define this joint probability, the generative model requires the enumeration of all possible observation sequences. Building such an extensive training set in a low privileged language like Bengali, is impractical.

Moreover, HMM assumes that the observation sequence is a set of isolated and independent observation units. In most applications such assumption is intractable as the observation units often are dependent based on several different features.

Maximum Entropy Markov Model (MEMM) addresses all the above problems. It defines the conditional probability P(**Y** | **X**) instead of joint probability. Moreover, for each source state it takes observation features as input and outputs a distribution over next possible states. However, it suffers from a problem called *label bias*. MEMM transitions leaving a particular state only compete against each other instead of competing globally across all the transitions. As a result, it creates a bias towards state with fewer outgoing transitions.

CRF, resolves both of the above problems. It works on the conditional probability P(**Y** | **X**). Therefore, it does not require any modelling effort on observation sequence. Moreover, unlike MEMM, which uses a per-state exponential model, CRF has a single exponential model for the joint probability of entire sequence of states for the given observation sequence. Hence it does not suffer from label bias problem.

CRF can be represented as an undirected graph that represent the conditional probability of the state sequence $\mathbf{Y} = \{y_1, y_2, ..., y_T\}$, for a given observation sequence $\mathbf{X} = \{x_1, x_2, \ldots, x_T\}$, as depicted below:

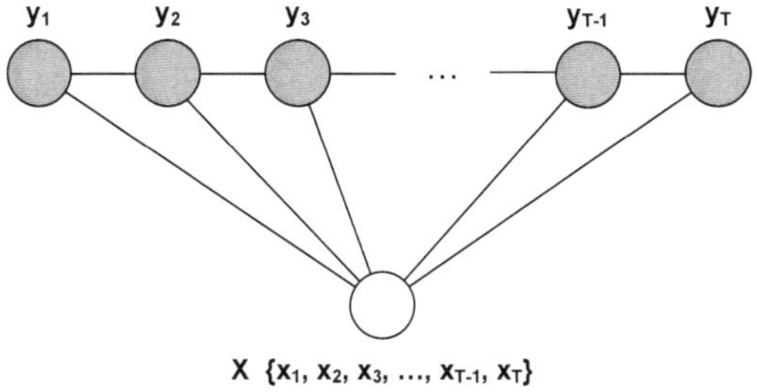

Figure 1: Graphical Structure of CRF

CRF makes a first-order Markov assumption on the state sequence – as the adjacent pair of state nodes (y_{t-1}, y_t) are linked by an undirected edge of the graph. However, it makes no assumption on the observation nodes, which is represented as a single node above.

3.1 Definition

We adopted the definition of CRF provided by Vail et al. (2007). The conditional probability P(**Y** | **X**) can be defined as the normalized product of strictly positive real-valued potential functions. The potential functions are computed over the cliques of CRF graph. As depicted in Figure 1, the cliques consist of the adjacent pairs of states and the entire observation sequence. Thus a potential function can be defined as $\psi(t, y_{t-1}, y_t, X)$, where t is an index in the state sequence. Since CRF is log-linear model (Wallach, 2004), the potential functions can be defined as follows:

$$\psi(t, y_{t-1}, y_t, X) = \exp(w^T, f(t, y_{t-1}, y_t, X))$$

Expression 1: Potential Function

where w presents a vector of weights and f is the vector of feature functions. The weight vector is estimated during training.

We define feature functions based on real-valued features. An example of a feature b from our area of application can be:

$$b(t, X) = \begin{cases} 1, \text{if } \mathrm{x_t} = \text{a particular surface word} \\ 0, \text{otherwise} \end{cases}$$

Expression 2: Feature

Thus we can define a feature function as following:

$$f(t, y_{t-1}, y_t, X) = \begin{cases} b(t, X), \text{if } \mathrm{y_{t-1}} = \mathrm{S_1} \text{ and } \mathrm{y_t} = \mathrm{S_2} \\ 0, \text{otherwise} \end{cases}$$

Expression 3: Feature Function

where S_1 and S_2 are two example stems.

Going by the previous definition of the conditional probability,

$$P(Y|X) = \frac{1}{Z} \prod_{t=1}^{T} \exp(w^T, f(t, y_{t-1}, y_t, X))$$

Expression 4: CRF Conditional Probability

where Z is the normalization constant. The strictly positive real-valued potential functions are not guaranteed to satisfy the axioms of probability. Thus Z is used to ensure that the summation of all the probability is equal to 1. Z is defined as below:

$$Z = \sum_{Y} \prod_{t=1}^{T} \exp(w^T, f(t, y_{t-1}, y_t, X))$$

Expression 5: CRF Normalisation Factor

3.2 Training

CRF training is actually about estimation of the weight vector w, where the conditional likelihood of the training corpus, which is labelled with states. Maximizing the conditional likelihood can be approximately equated to maximization of the log-likelihood, which is more convenient to achieve. Thus we define the log-likelihood as:

$$L(Y|X; w) = \sum_{t=1}^{T} w^T f(t, y_{t-1}, y_t, X) - \log(Z)$$

Expression 6: CRF Objective Function

The gradient of the above function is:

$$\frac{dL}{dw_i} = \sum_{t=1}^{T} f_i(t, y_{t-1}, y_t, X) - \sum_{Y} P(Y|X) f_i(t, y_{t-1}, y_t, X)$$

Expression 7: CRF Objective Function Gradient

Expression 6 is called the objective function. Optimization techniques (e.g. conjugate gradient, BFGS etc.) can be applied on the objective function to calculate the maximum log-likelihood.

3.3 Regularisation

Regularization norms can be applied on the above maximum likelihood calculation. Usually in CRF two different regularization norms are applied – L_1 and L_2.

In L_1 norm, instead of maximizing the log-likelihood alone a penalty term for each weight proportionate to $|w_i|$ are deducted from it. Thus the penalized objective function can be defined as below:

$$\max_{w} L(Y|X;w) - \mu\sum_{i}|w_i|$$

Expression 8: L_1 Norm

where μ a parameter that controls the degree of smoothing.

In L_2 norm, the penalty term is proportionate to w_i^2. The penalized objective function can be defined as below:

$$\max_{w} L(Y|X;w) - \mu w^T w$$

Expression 9: L2 Norm

4 Experiment

4.1 Corpora

We used two corpora for the experiment:

1. **Classic Literature Corpus (CLC)**. This corpus comprised of first five short stories (ঘাটের কথা [*ghaaTer kathaa*], রাজপথের কথা [*raajapather kathaa*], মুকুট [*mukuT*], দেনাপাওনা [*denaapaaonaa*], and পোস্টমাস্টার [*posTamaasTaar*]) by Rabindranath Tagore [Tagore 1960]. It was written in traditional and colloquial dialects. It contained 15,347 tokens. We ourselves hand-tagged the corpus with POS.
2. **Contemporary Travelogue Corpus (CTC)**. This corpus comprised of four travelogues (আমাজনের গাছবাড়ি [*aamaajaner gaach-habaarhi*], বক্সা-জয়ন্তী [*baksaa-jayantee*], বনসুন্দর [*banasundar*] and বাগান [*baagaan*]) from contemporary travel magazines. It was written in colloquial dialects. It contained 11,561 tokens. The corpus is POS tagged by Indian Languages to Indian Languages Machine Translation System (IL-ILMT) developed by Jadavpur University as part of a DIT funded project. The corpus is also POS tagged by us again manually.

4.2 Strategy

We devised the following experiment strategy:

- The biggest benefit of statistical approach is language independence. Hence the CRF must not be training with any linguistic details, to avoid infusing language dependency.
- Train a CRF system so that it can discover the sequence of stems (**Y**) from the test corpus based on the following observation sequence (**X**)
  - UNI: Surface word only
  - POS: A combination of surface word and POS of the surface word
- Run the CRF system on both CLC and CTC corpora to observe the performance on different domains.
- Test the domain affinity, if any, of the CRF system. For that we decided to test CTC corpus using CRF trained using CLC and vice versa.

4.3 Experiment Setup

Since CRF is a supervised learning technique, we crafted two sets of corpora – for training (CLC_L and CTC_L) and test (CLC_T and CTC_T) purpose respectively. The details about these corpora are provided in the table below:

Table 1: Corpora Used in CRF Experiment

Detail	Value
# Surface Words in CLC_L	8953
# Surface Words in CTC_L	7493
# Inflections in CLC_L	192
# Inflections in CTC_L	131
# Stems in CLC_L	1650
# Stems in CTC_L	1856
# Surface Words in CLC_T	9607
# Surface Words in CTC_T	4410

Additionally, we also created combined corpora – $Combined_L$ and $Combined_T$ respectively by joining the two corpora from respective sets.

We chose CRF++ (Taku-ku, 2003), an open source implementation of CRF developed using C++ language. CRF++ takes few parameters, of which we used a couple, which are described below:

- Regularization Norm: We chose L_2.
- Regularization Parameter (μ): We chose 1.0 as value.

CRF++ requires an input file for both training and testing. The format of this file is like a table where each record is a set of fields, which carry individual semantics. It can have multiple input fields followed by a single output field. The usage of input fields depend on the features used in the model – potentially some input fields may remain unused. We defined two input fields: surface word (F_1), and POS of the surface word (F_2).

We had two options for the output column – stem or inflection. The natural output of a stemmer is stem. Thus initially we went for it. However, when we tried to train it on a 4 GB i5 quad-core Windows 7 64-bit laptop, the CRF++ tool crashed. We did an analysis to discover the reason behind it as explained below.

As explained earlier, CRF++ generates feature functions ($f(t, y_{t-1}, y_t, X)$) based on the training records and the features defined. The feature functions are a combination of features, records and output classes. Hence the number of feature functions generated by the tool can be estimated as N*M*K, where N = number of features, M = number of records in training file and K = number of output classes. We defined one feature (N) and used CLC_L as training corpus, which contained 8953 surface words (M) and 1650 stems (K). Hence it generated more than 14 million feature functions (1 * 8953 * 1650 = 14,772,450). Obviously, the configuration of the laptop used was not powerful enough to handle it. Soon, as the performance monitoring revealed, the training task consumed all 4 GB of available primary memory, and resulted in a crash of CRF++.

Next, the second output class option, which was inflection, was considered. In a stemmer, the inflection is not the final output. However, for evaluation purpose of the statistical approach, it would serve well.

The number of feature functions estimated for CLC_L was around 1.7 million (1 * 8953 * 193 = 1,718,976), which is less than previous estimate by at least one order of magnitude. CRF++ could manage to run it successfully with a decent memory usage, even though the CPU usage hit the 100% limit with regular valleys. A typical resource utilization pattern of the machine during training was shown in Figure 2:

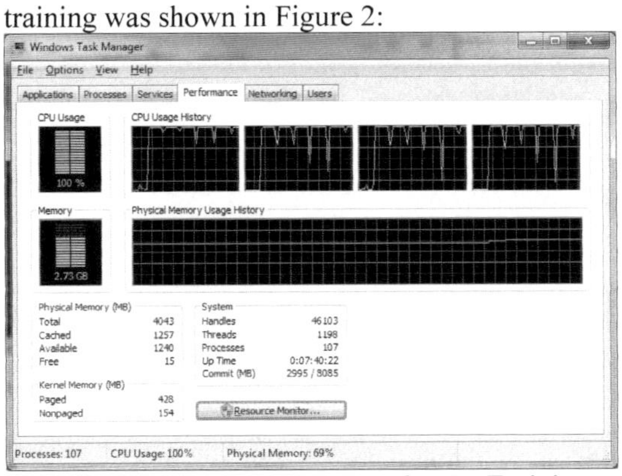

Figure 2: Machine Performance for the Training with Inflection as Output Class

In CRF++, the features (please refer to Expression 2) are defined in a template file. As we strategised, two different features, which do not have any linguistic details, were defined for two different experiment runs. They are defined below:

$$b_{UNI}(t, X) = \begin{cases} 1, \text{if } F_1 = \text{surface word of } x_t \\ 0, \text{otherwise} \end{cases}$$

Expression 10: Feature UNI

$$b_{POS}(t, X) = \begin{cases} 1, \text{if } F_1 = \text{surface word of } x_t \text{ and } F_2 = \text{POS of } x_t \\ 0, \text{otherwise} \end{cases}$$

Expression 11: Feature POS

5 Result

We trained the machine six times using different training corpora and features as summarized below:

Table 2: CRF Trained Models

Model	Training Corpus	Feature
TAGORE.UNI	CLC_L	UNI
TRAVEL.UNI	CTC_L	UNI
COMBINED.UNI	$Combined_L$	UNI
TAGORE.POS	CLC_L	POS
TRAVEL.POS	CTC_L	POS
COMBINED.POS	$Combined_L$	POS

We executed a set of test runs using different combinations of model and test corpus. Afterwards we compared the machine output with the manually determined gold standard and computed the accuracy. Following table presents the outcome:

Table 3: Accuracies Achieved in CRF Test Runs

Run	Model	Corpus	Result
CLC.TAGORE.UNI	TAGORE.UNI	CLC_T	84.7%
CTC.TAGORE.UNI	TAGORE.UNI	CTC_T	69.5%
CTC.TRAVEL.UNI	TRAVEL.UNI	CTC_T	79.8%
CLC.COMBINED.UNI	COMBINED.UNI	CLC_T	86.0%
CTC.COMBINED.UNI	COMBINED.UNI	CTC_T	81.6%
CLC.TAGORE.POS	TAGORE.POS	CLC_T	84.3%
CTC.TAGORE.POS	TAGORE.POS	CTC_T	68.2%
CTC.TRAVEL.POS	TRAVEL.POS	CTC_T	78.7%
CLC.COMBINED.POS	COMBINED.POS	CLC_T	85.6%
CTC.COMBINED.POS	COMBINED.POS	CTC_T	80.9%

Overall, the performance of the CRF stemmer is encouraging as it more or less consistently achieved an accuracy of more than 80%. It performed better than two other statistical stemmers

(Dasgupta and Ng, 2006; and Das and Bandyopadhyay, 2010), which reported 64.62% and 74.06% accuracy respectively for Bengali text.

We further analysed it on three different aspects as presented in the subsections below:

5.1 Effect of Features

We plotted different test runs to compare the effect of different features.

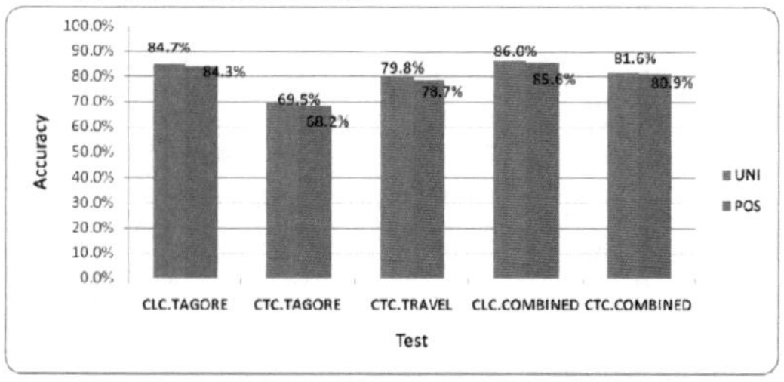

Figure 3: Effect of Features on Accuracy

As evident from above, having an additional feature in the form of POS, did not help the performance of the CRF stemmer. For all test runs, both of these features yielded almost similar performance.

5.2 Effect of Domains

We analyzed the effect of domains both on training and test corpus. We picked up the UNI feature based results as that was slightly better than POS based accuracies. The chart below depicts the result of this analysis:

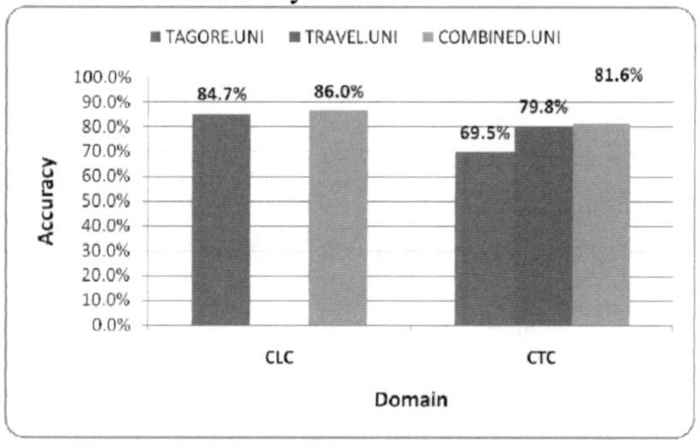

Figure 4: Effect of Domains on Accuracy

We made the following observation:

- CTC performed worse than CLC. We found that there were many spelling mistakes and malformed words present in this corpus. The CRF failed to find the right inflection pattern for such words.
- The performance of CTC against the model TAGORE.UNI produced worst result when compared against other runs of CTC. It shows that the statistical stemmer shows domain affinity. In this case the training and test corpus were from different domains – and that was the reason for bad accuracy.
- The combined model (COMBINED.UNI) yielded better performance than the respective trained models of domains. This observation matches the intuition that richness of the training data may improve the stemmer performance.

5.3 Rule-based vs. Statistical

In our survey, we could not find any work that compared the performances rule-based and statistical stemmers in the context of Bengali text. As third analysis step, we attempted the same.

We picked up the rule-based stemmer Mulaadhaar3 (M3) proposed by Sarkar and Bandyopadhyay (2012). M3 performances were reported on same set of test corpora, thus a fair comparison was possible. We compared the best results CRF achieved against the A_1 and A_2 accuracy measures of M3. The analysis result is depicted below:

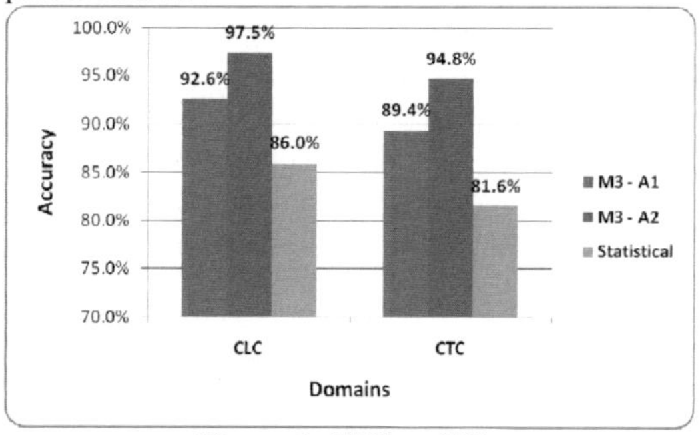

Figure 5: CRF vs. M3

As evident from above, M3 outperformed CRF on all the domains.

6 Conclusion

We tried a different statistical approach than the more popular options, in the form of a CRF based machine learning technique to produce a statistical stemmer for Bengali. The results found to be encouraging while comparing against other published works on Bengali statistical stemmers. However, we found that the rule-based stemmer M3 performed far better than the CRF stemmers.

However, the approach presented here is language independent. Thus it can be applied to languages where the deep linguistic rules are not yet formalised. It would be interesting to see its application in other Indo-Aryan languages like Oriya, Assamese etc. where linguistic rule-based stemmers are yet to arrive.

References

M. Bacchin, N. Ferro, and M. Melucci. 2002. *Experiments to evaluate a statistical stemming algorithm*. Proceedings of the Conference and Labs of the Evaluation Forum (CLEF).

M. Bacchin , N. Ferro, and M. Melucci. 2005. *A probabilistic model for stemmer generation*. Information Processing & Management, 41(1): 121-137.

B. Aisha, and M. Sun. 2009. *A Uyghur Morpheme Analysis Method based on Conditional Random Fields*. International Journal on Asian Language Processing, 19(2):69- 77.

N. L. Bhamidipati, and S. K. Pal. 2007. *Stemming via Distribution-Based Word Segregation for Classification and Retrieva*. IEEE Transactions on Systems, Man, and Cybernatics - Part B: Cybernatics, Vol. 37, No. 2.

J. H. Brits. 2006. *Outomatiese Setswana lemmaidentifisering*. Master's Thesis. North-West University, Potchefstroom, South Africa.

W.B. Croft, and J. Xu. 1995. *Corpus-Specific Stemming using Word Form Co-occurrences*. In Fourth Annual Symposium on Document Analysis and Information Retrieval.

A. Culotta, D. Kulp and A. McCallum. 2005. *Gene Prediction with Conditional Random Fields*. Technical Report UM-CS-2005-028, University of Massachusetts, Amherst.

A. Das, and S. Bandyopadhyay. 2010. *Morphological Stemming Cluster Identification for Bangla*. Knowledge Sharing Event-1: Task 3: Morphological Analyzers and Generators.

S. Dasgupta, and V. Ng. 2006. *Unsupervised Morphological Parsing for Bengali*. Language Resources and Evaluation, Volume 40, Numbers 3-4, 311-330.

U. Garain, and A. K. Datta. 2005. *An approach for stemming in symbolically compressed Indian language imaged documents*. Proceedings of the Eighth International Conference on Document Analysis and Recognition.

A. Gelbukh, M. Alexandrov, and S. Y. Han. 2004. *Detecting Inflection Patterns in Natural Language by Minimization of Morphological Model*. Progress in Pattern Recognition, Image Analysis and Applications: Lecture Notes in Computer Science, Volume 3287/2004, pp. 110-14.

J. A. Goldsmith, D. Higgins, and S. Soglasnova. 2001. *Automatic Language-Specific Stemming in Information Retrieval*. Cross-Language Information Retrieval and Evaluation String Processing and Information Retrieval: Lecture Notes in Computer Science, Volume 2857/2003, pp. 238-251.

H. J. Groenewald. 2009. *Using Technology Transfer to Advance Automatic Lemmatisation for Setswana*. Proceedings of the EACL 2009 Workshop on Language Technologies for African Languages – AfLaT 2009, pp. 32–37.

H. Hammarström. 2006. *Poor Man's Stemming: Unsupervised Recognition of Same-Stem Words*. Information Retrieval Technology: Lecture Notes in Computer Science, Volume 4182/2006, 323-337.

C. Jordan, J. Healy, and V. Keselj. 2005. *Swordfish: Using Ngrams in an Unsupervised Approach to Morphological Analysis*. Proceedings of Morpho Challenge.

L. S. Larkey, M. E. Connell, and N. Abduljaleel. 2003. *Hindi CLIR in Thirty Days*. ACM Transaction on Asian Language Information Processing, Vol-2, No. 2, pp. 130-142.

V. Levenshtein. 1966. *Binary codes capable of correcting deletions, insertions, and reversals*. Soviet Physics Doklady, 10: 707–10.

P. Majumder, M. Mitra, S. Parui, G. Kole, P. Mitra and K. Datta. 2007. *YASS: Yet another suffix stripper*. ACM Transactions on Information Systems (TOIS).

J. Mayfield, and P. McNamee. 2003. *Single N-gram Stemming*. Proceedings of the 26th Annual International ACM SIGIR Conference on Research and Development in Information Retrieval (SIGIR '03).

M. Melucci, and N. Orio. 2003. *A Novel Method for Stemmer Generation Based on Hidden Markov Models*. Proceedings of the twelfth international conference on Information and knowledge management (CIKM '03).

A. K. Pandey, and T. J. Siddiqui. 2008. *An Unsupervised Hindi stemmer with heuristic improvements*. Proceedings of the second workshop on Analytics for noisy unstructured text data (AND'08).

P. Patel, K. Popat, and P. Bhattacharyya. 2010. *Hybrid Stemmer for Gujarati*. Proceedings of the 1st Workshop on South and Southeast Asian Natural Language Processing (WSSANLP), The 23rd International Conference on Computational Linguistics (COLING), pp. 51–55.

M. F. Porter. 1980. *An algorithm for suffix stripping.* Program, 14(3):130-137.

A. Ramanathan, and D. D. Rao. 2003. *A Lightweight Stemmer for Hindi.* Proceedings of the 10th Conference of the European Chapter of the Association for Computational Linguistics.

H. Schmid. 1994. *Probabilistic part-of-speech tagging using decision trees.* Proceedings of International Conference on New Methods in Language Processing.

H. Tseng, P. Chang, G. Andrew, D. Jurafsky, and C. Manning . 2005. *A Conditional Random Field Word Segmenter.* Proceedings of the Fourth SIGHAN Workshop on Chinese Language Processing.

D. L. Vail, J. D. Lafferty, and M. M. Veloso. 2007. *Feature selection in conditional random fields for activity recognition.* Proceedings of the International Conference on Intelligent Robots and Systems (IROS 2007).

Y. Wang, K. F. Loe, and J. K. Wu. 2006. *A dynamic conditional random field model for foreground and shadow segmentation.* IEEE Transactions on Pattern Analysis and Machine Intelligence, 28(2), pp. 279-189.

S. Sarkar, and S. Bandyopadhyay. 2012. *Mulaadhaar: Towards an Improved Stemmer and Its Effect on Machine Tagged Travelogue Corpus.* International Journal of Computational Linguistics and Natural Language Processing, Volume 1, Issue 5.

Taku-ku. 2003. *CRF++: Yet Another CRF toolkit.* [Online] Accessed on 11 Jun 2013 at http://crfpp.googlecode.com/svn/trunk/doc/index.html

Urdu Hindi Machine Transliteration using SMT

M. G. Abbas Malik
Faclty of Computing and IT
NJB
King Abdulaziz University,
Saudi Arabia
mgmalik@kau.edu.sa

Christian Boitet
GETALP – LIG
University of Grenoble, France
Christian.boitet@imag.fr

Laurent Besacier
GETALP – LIG
University of Grenoble, France
Laurent.Besacier@imag.fr

Pushpak Bhattcharyya
Indian Institute of Technology
Bombay, India
pb@iitb.ac.in

Abstract

Transliteration is a process of transcribing a word of the source language into the target language such that when the native speaker of the target language pronounces it, it sounds as the native pronunciation of the source word. Statistical techniques have brought significant advances and have made real progress in various fields of Natural Language Processing (NLP). In this paper, we have analysed the application of Statistical Machine Translation (SMT) for solving the problem of Urdu Hindi transliteration using a parallel lexicon. We have designed total 24 Statistical Transliteration (ST) systems by combining different types of *alignments*, *translation models* and *target language models*. We have performed total 576 experiments and have reported significant results. From Hindi–to–Urdu transliteration, we have achieved the maximum word-level accuracy of 71.5%. From Urdu–to–Hindi transliteration, the maximum word-level accuracy is 77.8% when the input Urdu text contains all necessary diacritical marks and 77% when the input Urdu text does not contain all necessary diacritical marks. At character-level, transliteration accuracy is more than 90% in both directions.

1 Introduction

Hindi is the national language of India. Urdu is the national language of Pakistan and is also one of the official languages of India. Urdu and Hindi are also considered as two dialects of the same language, called 'Hindustani' (Platts 1909), because of their common grammatical and linguistic structure (Rai 2000; Khan 2006). In the words of (Rai 2000), "One man's Hindi is another man's Urdu". In addition to the lexical differences, the other main difference between Urdu and Hindi is their writing systems. Urdu is written in a derived *Persio-Arabic* script and Hindi is written in the *Devanagari* script. Whether Hindi and Urdu are two different languages or not, they jointly represent the 2nd largest population of the world, including 1st and 2nd language speakers, after Chinese. This is shown in Table 1 (all figures are in millions).

	Native Speakers	2nd Language Speakers	Total
Hindi	366.00	487.00	853.00
Urdu	60.29	104.00	164.29
Total	426.29	591.00	**1,017.29**

Table 1: Size of Urdu and Hindi (Rahman 2004; Lewis 2009)

Empiricism was a prominent trend in computational linguistics in the 1940s and 50s. This trend was discouraged by Chomsky's claim that statistical approaches will always suffer from data scarcity and as a result radical approaches were more dominant for more than a decade. Empiricism re-emerged with the successful use of probabilistic models and Hidden Markov

Model (HMM) by the *speech recognition* group at CMU (Harpy system) and IBM in the 1970s (Rabiner and Juang 1986; Rabinder 1989). Statistical approaches have brought significant advances and have made real progress in various fields of Natural Language Processing (NLP), like word sense disambiguation, POS tagging, information retrieval and especially Statistical Machine Translation (SMT) (Brown et al. 1990; Brown et al. 1993; Koehn et al. 2007; Lopez 2008; Koehn 2010), where the sense of real progress is the most visible on Internet. Statistical approaches are data-driven, and the sparsity of data is indeed a major problem for Statistical language processing, especially for under-resourced languages or language pairs.

Transliteration is a process of transcribing a word of the source language into the target language such that when the native speaker of the target language pronounces it, it sounds as the native pronunciation of the source word. Statistical approaches, especially SMT, are getting attention of researchers for solving the problems of transliteration (Knight and Graehl 1997; Lee and Choi. 1998; Stall and Knight 1998; Al-Onaizan and Knight 2002; AbdulJaleel and Larkey 2003; Li, Zhang and Su 2004; Ekbal, Naskar and Bandyopadhyay 2006; Finch and Sumita 2009; Kirschenbaum and Wintner 2009; Malik et al. 2009; Nabende 2009; Durrani et al. 2010). Malik et al. (2009) used a hybrid transliteration model for *Urdu–to–Hindi* transliteration. They replaced the translation model of the classical SMT by a rule-based non-deterministic transducer and used the Hindi language model to select the best transliteration. They reported an accuracy of 79.1%. Durrani et al. (2010) used a conditional probability model (M1) and a joint probability model (M2) for *Hindi–to–Urdu* translation. They incorporated their character-based transliteration model learnt from Urdu – Hindi parallel word list into Models M1 and M2. They reported very low BLUE scores of 19.35 and 18.34 for models M1 and M2 respectively.

We have developed statistical models for solving the problem of Urdu ↔ Hindi transliteration (bidirectional) using an Urdu – Hindi parallel word list resource, extracted from the data of a dictionary of Urdu, classical Hindi and English (Platts 1884) [1], digitized under the project "Digital South Asian Library" at University of Chicago, USA[2] and Center for Research Libraries[3].

In this paper, we have discussed our training data, the Urdu – Hindi parallel lexicon in Section 2. Various components of Statistical Transliteration (ST) systems like data alignment techniques, transliteration models and target language models are discussed in Section 3. 24 ST systems for Urdu – Hindi transliteration are described in Section 4. In Section 5, we have described the experimental setup and discussed the results of our tests. Finally the conclusion of the paper is given.

2 Training Data

Urdu – Hindi is an under-resourced language pair. The Digital South Asian Library (DSAL) has digitized "A Dictionary of Urdu, classical Hindi and English" (Platts 1884). The originally published dictionary includes the Urdu/Persio-Arabic transcriptions of all word entries, while it contains Hindi/Devanagari transcriptions only for words that are not of Persio-Arabic origin. The original DSAL dictionary data that we received in March 2007, did not contain the Urdu word transcriptions in the Persio-Arabic script, instead it contained their Roman transcriptions[4]. Two sample entries in the original DSAL's dictionary data are shown in Figure 1. We are particularly interested by the highlighted areas of these entries.

```
<div2 type="article"
id="ābādī"><head><hi>ābādī</hi></head><p><p>P
<pa>ābādī</pa> <i>ābādī</i>, s.f. Inhabited spot or place; colo-
ny; population, number of inhabitants; cultivated
place;cultivation; the part of a village lands brought under culti-
vation; increased assessment (=<i>beshī</i>); prosperity; stateof
comfort; happiness, joy, pleasure.</p></div2>
<div2 type="article" id="अबार_abār"><head><hi>अबार
abār</hi></head><p><p>H <pa>abār</pa> अबार <i>abār</i>
[S. अवार], s.m. This side, the nearbank of a river.</p></div2>
```

Figure 1: Sample entries in the DSAL dictionary

The silver highlighting ('id=') contains only the Roman transcription instead of the Urdu transcription of the word entry (1st sample entry), when the word is of Persio-Arabic origin, otherwise it contains the Hindi/Devanagari transcription '_' Roman transcription for the word entry (2nd sample entry). Each word entry has 'hi' and 'pa' tags for Hindi/Devanagari and Urd/Persio-Arabic transcriptions respectively. The format of the data is not strictly XML-based, but contains certain tags like 'hi' and 'pa'.

From this raw data, we extracted the Roman transcription and its Hindi/Devanagari transcrip-

[1] http://dsal.uchicago.edu/dictionaries/platts/

[2] http://dsal.uchicago.edu/

[3] http://www.crl.edu/

[4] The current online version contains Urdu/Persio-Arabic transcription, updated in August, 2008.

tion (if present) for each word entry. After an exhaustive analysis of the extracted Roman transcriptions, we built a finite-state transducer that can convert these Roman transcriptions into the Urdu/Persio-Arabic and Hindi/Devanagari (if not existed) transcriptions. In this way, we developed an Urdu – Hindi parallel lexicon containing total 55,253 words. We used 50,000 Urdu – Hindi parallel words as training data to build our statistical transliteration models for Urdu – Hindi machine transliteration. The remaining 5,253 Urdu – Hindi parallel words were used for testing and tuning purposes.

3 Statistical Transliteration (ST)

Following the classical Statistical Machine Translation (SMT) techniques, first we develop *alignments* between the parallel data. The only difference between a classical SMT system and our Statistical Transliteration (ST) system is the parallel data. In SMT, the parallel data consist of parallel sentences; In ST, it consists of parallel words. Examples of Urdu – Hindi parallel words are shown in Table 2 with their International Phonetic Alphabet (IPA) transcriptions and English glosses.

Hindi	Urdu with diacritics	Urdu without diacritics	IPA	English
अब्बा	اَبّا	ابا	əbbɑ	Father
इबलाग़	اِبلاغ	ابلاغ	ɪbəlɑx	Conveying
उबलाना	اُبلانا	ابلانا	ʊbəlɑnɑ	To boil
इबलीस	اِبلِیس	ابلیس	ɪbəlis	Devil
अभागेपन	ابھاگیپن	ابھاگیپن	əb^{h}ɑgepən	Unfortunate
अप्रैल	اَپْرَیل	اپریل	əpræl	April
अच्छा	اَچّھا	اچھا	ətʃtʃɑ	Good

Table 2: Sample Urdu – Hindi parallel lexical entries

The Urdu words that we have generated from the Roman transcriptions from the DSAL dictionary data contain all required diacritical marks, clearly shown in Table 2. Diacritical marks are the back bone of the Urdu vowel system and they are mandatory for the correct pronunciation of an Urdu word, as well as Urdu computational linguistics (Zia 1999). Like in Arabic, diacritical marks are sparingly used in written Urdu (Zia 1999). To model this unfortunate situation, we developed another Urdu – Hindi parallel lexicon by removing all diacritics from the fully diacritized Urdu words, also shown in Table 2. In this way, we developed two types of Hindi – Urdu parallel data.

From these parallel Urdu – Hindi entries, we developed two types of alignments. Secondly, we developed *transliteration models* based on the alignments and *language models* based on monolingual Urdu and Hindi corpus. Finally, we joined these models to perform Urdu ↔ Hindi bidirectional transliteration.

3.1 Alignments

We developed two types of alignments that are discussed in the following two sections:

3.1.1 Character alignments

We can align the data at *character-level* by considering each Hindi – Urdu parallel word pair as a parallel sentence pair like classical SMT and each character in the parallel entry as a word. For *character alignments*, a space is introduced after each character in the Urdu (whether diacritized or not) and Hindi words in Urdu – Hindi parallel lexicons. Table 3 shows sample Urdu – Hindi parallel data for character alignments.

Hindi	Urdu with diacritics	Urdu without diacritics
अ ब ◌् ब	ا ب ◌ّ ا	ا ب ا
इ ब ल ◌ा ग़	ا ◌ِ ب ل ا غ	ا ب ل ا غ
उ ब ल ◌ा न ◌ा	ا ◌ُ ب ل ا ن ا	ا ب ل ا ن ا
इ ब ल ◌ी स	ا ◌ِ ب ل ◌ِ ی س	ا ب ل ی س
अ भ ◌ा ग ◌े प न	ا ◌َ ب ھ ا گ ی پ ن	ا ب ھ ا گ ی پ ن
अ प ◌् र ◌ै ल	ا ◌َ پ ◌ْ ر ◌َ ی ل	ا پ ر ی ل
अ च ◌् छ ◌ा	ا ◌َ چ ھ ◌ّ ا	ا چ ھ ا

Table 3: Sample Urdu – Hindi parallel data for character alignment

From these two types of Urdu – Hindi parallel data, we developed two types of character alignments using GIZA++ (Och and Ney 2003) in both directions:

- Hindi and Urdu with diacritics character alignment,
- Hindi and Urdu without diacritics character alignment.

3.1.2 Cluster alignments

Alignment plays a critical role in SMT (Fraser and Marcu 2007; Kumar, Och and Macherey 2007; Huang 2009). The quality of parallel data and the word alignment have a significant impact on learning the translation model and consequently on the quality of the SMT system (Fraser and Marcu 2007; Huang 2009). It is always better do an analysis of the alignment and correct the alignment errors to reduce the Alignment Error Rate (AER).

We also analyzed the alignments produced by GIZA++. We found that we can improve our alignments to reduce the AER. The incorrect alignments are highlighted in Table 4 (below) that shows Hindi to Urdu with diacritics alignments of our sample words of Table 3.

The vowel representation in Urdu/Persio-Arabic script is highly complex and context-sensitive (Hussain 2004; Malik, Boitet and Bhattacharyya 2008; Malik et al. 2009). This highly complex and contextual representation leads to wrong character alignments, highlighted in Table 4. In the second row of Table 4, the Hindi vowel इ [ɪ] is aligned with ALEF (ا) and ZER (ِ) is aligned to NULL. The alignment is not completely incorrect, but the vowel इ [ɪ] must be aligned with both ALEF (ا) and ZER (ِ). Similarly, the Hindi vowel उ [ʊ] must be aligned with ALEF (ا) and PESH (ُ) in the third row. In these examples, one character in Hindi must be aligned with a sequence of characters in Urdu. Interestingly, we have observed that GIZA++ correctly aligns such cases for Urdu (with or without diacritics) to Hindi alignments.

1	# Sentence pair (6) source length 4 target length 5 alignment score : 1.70006e-05 अ ब ् ब ा NULL ([ ]) 5]) ا ([3]) ّ ([4 2]) ب ([1]) ا])
2	# Sentence pair (114) source length 6 target length 5 alignment score : 0.00032306 इ ब ल ा ग़ NULL ([ ])]) غ ([4]) ا ([3]) ل ([2]) ب ([ ]) ِ ([1]) ا 5])
3	# Sentence pair (115) source length 7 target length 6 alignment score : 0.000154595 उ ब ल ा न ा NULL ([ ])]) ن ([4]) ا ([3]) ل ([2]) ب ([ ]) ُ ([1]) ا 6]) ا ([5])
4	# Sentence pair (128) source length 7 target length 5 alignment score : 5.58545e-05 इ ब ल ी स NULL ([ ])]) ی ([ ]) ِ ([3]) ل ([2]) ب ([ ]) ِ ([1]) ا 5]) س ([4])
5	# Sentence pair (167) source length 9 target length 7 alignment score : 3.20243e-05 अ भ ा ग े प न NULL ([ ])]) ی ([4]) گ ([3]) ا ([ ]) ھ ([2]) ب ([1]) ا 7]) ن ([ ]) ´ ([6]) پ ([5])
6	# Sentence pair (464) source length 6 target length 6 alignment score : 7.74271e-06 अ प ् र ै ल NULL ([ ]) ل ([5]) ی ([3]) ُ ([4]) ر ([2]) پ ([1]) ا 6])])
7	# Sentence pair (1183) source length 5 target length 5 alignment score : 3.13657e-05 अ च ् छ ा NULL ([ ]) 5]) ا ([3]) ّ ([4]) ھ ([2]) چ ([1]) ا])

Table 4: Character alignment examples from Hindi to Urdu with diacritics

All such vowel alignments can be improved by clustering the specific sequences of characters in the Urdu side.

In the case of consonants, we also observe a few alignment problems. In Urdu, *gemination* of a consonant is marked with a SHADDA (ّ), while in Hindi, it is written as a *conjunct* form. The highlighted alignments of the first row of Table 4 align the Hindi characters ब [b] and ् with the Urdu characters BEH (ب) and SHADDA (ّ) respectively. Again this alignment is not completely wrong, but this geminated consonant alignment problem is more evident for Urdu to Hindi alignment where a Hindi consonant is aligned with NULL. An example of Urdu to Hindi alignment is shown in Table 5. This problem can be resolved by clustering the gemination representations both in Urdu and Hindi.

Sentence pair (754) source length 9 target length 10 alignment score : 8.0263e-13 اِ تّ ف ا ق اً NULL ([9]) इ ([1 2]) त ([3]) ् ([4]) त ([ ]) ि ([5]) फ़ ([6]) ा ([7]) क़ ([8]) न ([10])

Table 5. Gemination alignment from Urdu to Hindi

We also observe alignment problems for aspirated consonants because they are represented by a sequence of characters in Urdu and by either a single character or a sequence of characters in Hindi. For Hindi to Urdu alignment, this problem is highlighted in row 5 and 7 of Table 4. For Urdu to Hindi alignment, an example is shown in Table 6.

Sentence pair (1183) source length 5 target length 5 alignment score : 8.57561e-05 ا چ ھّ ا NULL ([ ]) अ ([1]) च ([2]) ् ([ ]) छ ([3 4]) ा ([5])

Table 6. Aspirated consonant alignment from Urdu to Hindi

All these problems increase the AER. Thus we decided to cluster certain character sequences in Urdu – Hindi parallel lexical entries to enhance the alignments and consequently transliteration between Urdu and Hindi. For clustering, we developed finite-state transducers that generate Urdu – Hindi clustered parallel lexicons. Clustered Urdu – Hindi parallel lexicons for our sample data of Table 2 with IPAs are shown in Table 7.

Hindi	Urdu with diacritics	IPA	Urdu without diacritics	IPA
अ ब्ब	ا بّ ا	ə bb ɑ	ا ب ا	ə b ɑ
इ ब ल ा ग़	اِ ب ل ا غ	ɪ b l ɑ x	ا ب ل ا غ	ə b l ɑ x
उ ब ल ा न ा	اُ ب ل ا ن ا	ʊ b l ɑ n ɑ	ا ب ل ا ن ا	ə b l ɑ n ɑ
इ ब ल ी स	اِ ب ل ی س	ɪ b l i s	ا ب ل ی س	ə b l e s
अ भ ा ग े प न	اَ بھ ا گ ی پ ن	ə bʰ ɑ g e pə n	ا بھ ا گ ی پ ن	ə bʰ ɑ g e pə n
अ प ् र ै ल	اَ پْ رَ ی ل	ə p r æ l	ا پ ر ی ل	ə p r e l
अ च्छ ा	اَ چھّ ا	ə ʧʧʰ ɑ	ا چھ ا	ə ʧʰ ɑ

Table 7: Sample clustered Urdu – Hindi lexical entries

Using these clustered Urdu – Hindi parallel lexical entries, we developed two types of *cluster alignments* using GIZA++ in both directions:

- Hindi and Urdu with diacritics cluster alignments
- Hindi and Urdu without diacritics cluster alignments

All the alignments problem discussed above are solved in cluster alignments as shown in Table 8.

1	# Sentence pair (6) source length 3 target length 3 alignment score : 0.0214204 अ ब्ब ा NULL ([ ]) 3]) ا ([2]) بّ ([1]) ا])
2	# Sentence pair (114) source length 5 target length 5 alignment score : 0.0942275 इ ब ल ा ग़ NULL ([ ]) 5]) غ ([4]) ا ([3]) ل ([2]) ب ([1]) اِ])
3	# Sentence pair (115) source length 6 target length 6 alignment score : 0.0373352 उ ब ल ा न ा NULL ([ ]) 5]) ن ([4]) ا ([3]) ل ([2]) ب ([1]) اُ 6]) ا ([ ])
4	# Sentence pair (128) source length 5 target length 5 alignment score : 0.0430949 इ ब ल ी स NULL ([ ])]) س ([4]) ی ([3]) ل ([2]) ب ([1]) اِ 5])
5	# Sentence pair (167) source length 8 target length 7 alignment score : 0.000313045 अ भ ा ग े प न NULL ([ ]) 5]) ی ([4]) گ ([3]) ا ([2]) بھ ([1]) ا 7]) ن ([ ]) َ ([6]) پ ([ ])
6	# Sentence pair (464) source length 5 target length 6 alignment score : 1.71945e-05 अ प ् र ै ल NULL ([3])]) ل ([5]) یَ ([4]) ر ([2]) پ ([1]) ا 6])
7	# Sentence pair (754) source length 8 target length 7 alignment score : 0.000371183 इ त्त ि फ़ ा क़ न NULL ([ ]) 5]) ا ([4]) ف ([3]) ِ ([2]) تّ ([1]) اِ 7]) ً ([ ]) ا ([6]) ق ([ ])
8	# Sentence pair (1183) source length 3 target length 3 alignment score : 0.0207299 अ च्छ ा NULL ([ ]) 3]) ا ([2]) چھّ ([1]) ا])

Table 8: Sample Urdu - Hindi cluster alignments

These better cluster alignments will turn out to help to learn a better quality transliteration model and to enhance the quality of our Urdu ↔ Hindi transliterations.

3.2 Transliteration/Translation Models

Based on the character and cluster alignments, we developed 8 Urdu – Hindi transliteration models (or translation models of classical SMT) using the Moses toolkit (Koehn et al. 2007).

1. **M1**: learned from Hindi to Urdu with diacritics character alignment
2. **M2**: learned from Hindi to Urdu without diacritics character alignment
3. **M3**: learned from Hindi to Urdu with diacritics cluster alignment
4. **M4**: learned from Hindi to Urdu without diacritics cluster alignment
5. **M5**: learned from Urdu with diacritics to Hindi character alignment

6. **M6**: learned from Urdu without diacritics to Hindi character alignment
7. **M7**: learned from Urdu with diacritics to Hindi cluster alignment
8. **M8**: learned from Urdu without diacritics to Hindi cluster alignment

For developing these transliteration models, we used the training script 'train-factored-phrase-model.perl' with options 'grow-diag-final' and 'msd-bidirectional-fe' (default options) for alignment and re-ordering respectively, to learn these models from different type of alignments.

3.3 Target Language Models

A *target language model* $P(e)$ is a probabilistic model that scores the well-formedness of different translation solutions produced by the translation model (Koehn, Och and Marcu 2003; Zens and Ney 2003; Och and Ney 2004; Al-Onaizan and Papineni 2006). It generates a probability distribution over possible sequences of words and computes the probability of producing a given word w_1 given all the words that precede it in the sentence (Al-Onaizan and Papineni 2006). We developed multiple target language models depending on the type of alignments used in the transliteration models and the target language. We broadly categorize them into *word language models* and *sentence language models*, discussed below.

3.3.1 Word Language Models (WLM)

A *word language model* is a 6-gram statistical model that gives a probability distribution over possible sequences of characters and computes the probability of producing a given character or cluster C1, given the 5 characters or clusters that precede it in the word. We developed Hindi – Urdu parallel lexicons for learning the various Hind – Urdu alignments and transliteration models. The target side words of the parallel lexicons are used to generate word language models using the SRILM freeware [5]. For example, we developed *Urdu Word Language Models with Diacritics* from our character and clustered Urdu words with diacritics, and used them as target language models with the corresponding transliteration model. We thus developed total 6 different word language models, 2 for Hindi (character-based & cluster-based) and 4 for Urdu.

[5] http://www.speech.sri.com/projects/srilm/

3.3.2 Sentence Language Models (SLM)

Similarly to a word language model, a sentence language model is also a 6-gram statistical model that computes the probability of producing a given character or cluster C1, given the 5 characters or clusters that precede it in the sentence. The Urdu – Hindi pair is an under-resourced pair, but there exist some monolingual corpora for both Urdu and Hindi.

For Hindi, a Hindi corpus of more than 3 million words is freely available at the "Resource Center for Indian Language Technology Solutions" of the Indian Institute of Technology Bombay (IITB)[6]. We processed this Hindi corpus and extracted a Hindi sentence corpus that contains one sentence per line, for a total of 173,087 Hindi sentences. From it, we developed a character-level Hindi corpus by introducing a space after each character and a cluster-level Hindi corpus by applying our Hindi clustering finite-state transducer on the character-level Hindi corpus. These two character-level and cluster-level Hindi corpora were used to develop character-level and cluster-level Hindi Sentence Language Models using the SRILM toolkit.

A monolingual Urdu corpus (Reference # ELRA-W0037) of more than 2 million words is also available from the "Evaluations and Language Resources Distribution Agency" (ELRA/ELDA)[7]. This corpus was developed under the EMILLE[8] project of Lancaster University, UK. Like the Hindi corpus, we processed this Urdu corpus and extracted from it an Urdu sentence corpus. It contains a total of 127,685 sentences. We developed a character-level and cluster-level Urdu corpus by introducing a space after each character and then by applying clustering. Finally, we developed character-level and cluster-level Urdu Sentence Language Models using the SRILM toolkit.

Similar to *word language model*, We have developed total 6 sentence language models, 2 for Hindi and 4 for Urdu. Another set of 6 target language models are developed by combining the corresponding word and sentence language models.

4 Statistical Transliteration Systems

We have developed total 8 transliteration models, 4 for Hindi–to–Urdu and 4 for Urdu–to–Hindi transliteration. We have also developed 18

[6] http://www.cfilt.iitb.ac.in/
[7] http://www.elda.org/
[8] http://www.emille.lancs.ac.uk/index.php

target side language models. By combining these transliteration and target language models, we have developed total 24 Urdu↔Hindi statistical transliteration systems, 12 for Hindi–to–Urdu and 12 for Urdu–to–Hindi transliteration.

For Hindi–to–Urdu transliteration, we have built 4 translation models based on different Hindi–Urdu alignments and 8 Urdu target language models, discussed above. In the Moses toolkit, we can direct the SMT system to use multiple target language models. Thus we built 4 other target language models by combining our *Urdu (with or without diacritics) word language models (character and cluster level)* and *Urdu sentence language models (character and cluster level)*. Hindi–to–Urdu statistical transliteration systems are shown in Figure 2.

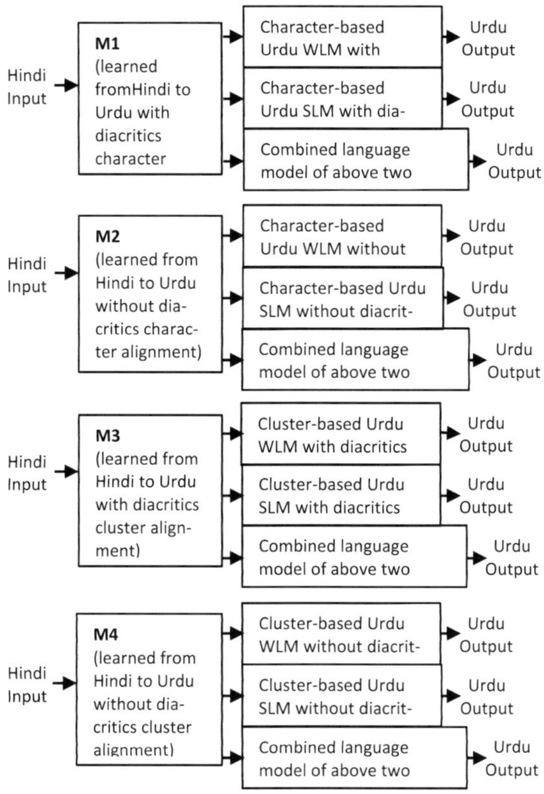

Figure 2: Hindi–to–Urdu Statistical Transliteration (ST) systems

We developed an Urdu – Hindi parallel lexicon containing total 55,253 words. 50,000 words were used to develop transliteration models and 2,500 for tuning each transliteration model. The remaining 2,753 Urdu – Hindi parallel words were used as Test Set 1 for testing purposes.

We also built 12 statistical transliteration systems for Urdu–to–Hindi transliteration. We developed 4 transliteration models based on different Urdu–Hindi alignments and 4 Hindi target language models. As for Hindi–to–Urdu transliteration, we combined *Hindi word language model* and *Hindi sentence language model*. Figure 3 shows different Urdu–to–Hindi statistical transliteration models.

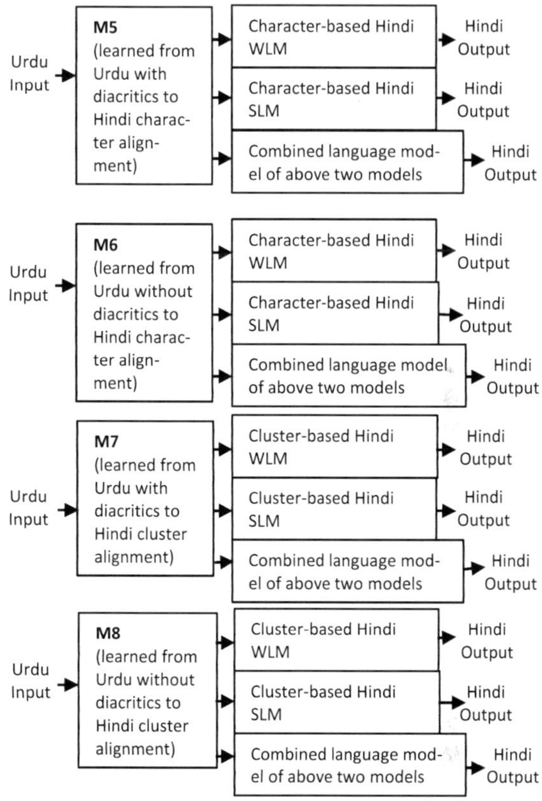

Figure 3: Figure 3: Urdu–to–Hindi Statistical Transliteration (ST) systems

5 Experiments and Results

Urdu – Hindi transliteration models are learnt from Urdu – Hindi parallel lexicons, thus the input to these Statistical Transliteration (ST) systems must be a word and not a running text or a sentence. The Hindi or Urdu input text is pre-processed to generate a list of Hindi or Urdu words before feeding it to the ST systems. The output of the ST systems is then post-processed to generate the final Urdu or Hindi output text.

5.1 Test Sets

We developed three Urdu – Hindi test sets. **Test Set 1** contains 2,753 Hindi–Urdu parallel words.

Test Set 2 contains 200 sentences (4,281 words) of Hindi origin that were extracted at random from a Hindi corpus of more than 3 million words. It is a common practice in the Hindi community to use the characters क [k], ख [k^h], ग [g], ज [ʤ], ड [ɖ], ढ [$ɖ^h$] and फ [p] instead of the characters क़ [q], ख़ [x], ग़ [ɣ], ज़ [z], ड़ [ɽ], ढ़ [$ɽ^h$] and फ़ [f] respectively, due to their shape similarities. In Test Set 2, the extracted Hindi sentences were edited and corrected for these typographical errors. Then, we translated the extracted Hindi sentences into Urdu by using an online Hindi–Urdu transliteration system[9]. These translated Urdu sentences were post-edited to remove errors, and all necessary diacritical marks were introduced in the Urdu text. Diacritical marks are vital for Urdu to Hindi transliteration, but they are sparingly used by people in writing. To compute the performance of our ST systems in this unfortunate but real situation, we developed another Urdu test data by removing the diacritical marks from the post-edited 200 Urdu sentences. These Hindi and Urdu (with and without diacritics) data served as input to our ST systems as well as an output reference for the automatic transliteration evaluations

Test Set 3 contains 226 sentences (4,632 words) of Urdu origin that were extracted at random from the Urdu corpus of more than 2 million words. To build Test Set 3, we first edited the extracted Urdu sentences for any error and restored the missing but necessary diacritics. We also developed a new Urdu test data without diacritics by removing all diacritical marks from the edited Urdu sentences. Then the edited Urdu sentences with diacritics were translated into Hindi using online an Urdu – Hindi transliteration system. The translated Hindi sentences were then post-edited for any error. These data are also used both as an input as well as a reference output.

5.2 Experiments

We experimented with 12 Hindi–to–Urdu and 12 Urdu–to–Hindi ST systems. Each ST system was tuned with 2,500 Urdu – Hindi parallel words using the Moses 'mert-moses.pl' script. Thus we have another set of 24 ST systems with tuning and it raises the total number of ST systems to 48. During the application of these ST systems on our difference test sets, we also varied the re-ordering parameter to analyse its effect on Urdu – Hindi ST systems. Again, this parameter varia-variation doubled the total number of our ST systems, from 48 to 96.

For Hindi–to–Urdu transliteration, we performed 96 experiments for each test set, that is in total 288 experiments. Each Urdu output was then post-processed (diacritics were removed) to compare it with Urdu references with and without diacritics.

For Urdu–to–Hindi transliteration, we have two types of inputs, with and without diacritics. Again, we conducted 288 Urdu–to–Hindi transliteration experiments, from which we computed character-level, word-level and sentence level accuracies.

5.3 Results and Discussion

Due to space limitation, we will only report and discuss the results of particular interest. We subdivide the results for each test set by the transliteration model, the alignment strategy, and the type of input/output data, because it is difficult to present all results in only one large table.

5.3.1 Hindi–to–Urdu transliteration results

Table 9 shows all the results of ST systems for Hindi–to–Urdu transliteration of transliteraiton models M1 and M2 for Test Set 2. The best results for M1 are 71.5% and 5.5% at the word-level and the sentence level respectively, shown in bold in the upper grid of Table 9. The best result at word-level and sentence level are produced by the ST systems *M1-Urdu SLM+ WLM-WD-No-Reordering* and *M1-Urdu SLM-No-Reordering* respectively.

[9] http://www.sanlp.org/HUMT/index.html

SMT Model	Sentence Accuracy		Word accuracy		Character accuracy	
	default output	Processed output	default output	processed output	default output	processed output
M1-Urdu WLM-WD-With-Reordering	0.5%	3%	26.1%	65.7%	89.1%	93.3%
M1-Urdu WLM-WD-No-Reordering	0.5%	3%	26.1%	65.7%	89.1%	93.3%
M1-Urdu WLM-WD-Tuned-With-Reordering	1%	3%	34.4%	62.9%	88.7%	92.7%
M1-Urdu WLM-WD-Tuned-No-Reordering	1%	3%	34.4%	62.9%	88.7%	92.7%
M1-Urdu SLM-WD-With-Reordering	1%	4%	48.9%	62.2%	84.9%	92.2%
M1-Urdu SLM-WD-No-Reordering	1%	**5.5%**	49.7%	64.2%	85.8%	93.3%
M1-Urdu SLM-WD-Tuned-With-Reordering	0.5%	3.5%	34.2%	63.3%	88.6%	92.6%
M1-Urdu SLM-WD-Tuned-No-Reordering	0.5%	3.5%	34.2%	63.3%	88.6%	92.6%
M1-Urdu SLM+WLM-WD-With-Reordering	1%	4.5%	50.5%	70.9%	89.0%	94.3%
M1-Urdu SLM+WLM-WD -No-Reordering	1%	4.5%	50.8%	**71.5%**	89.2%	**94.5%**
M1-Urdu SLM+WLM-WD -Tuned-With-Reordering	1%	3%	33.9%	62.7%	88.6%	92.6%
M1-Urdu SLM+WLM-WD -Tuned-No-Reordering	1%	3%	33.9%	62.7%	88.6%	92.6%
M2-Urdu WLM-WOD-With-Reordering	3%	3%	63.6%	63.6%	93.3%	93.3%
M2-Urdu WLM-WOD-No-Reordering	3%	3%	63.6%	63.6%	93.3%	93.3%
M2-Urdu WLM-WOD-Tuned-With-Reordering	3%	3%	64.8%	64.8%	92.6%	92.6%
M2-Urdu WLM-WOD-Tuned-No-Reordering	3%	3%	64.8%	64.8%	92.6%	92.6%
M2-Urdu SLM-WOD-With-Reordering	**5.5%**	**5.5%**	63.2%	63.2%	92.9%	92.9%
M2-Urdu SLM-WOD-No-Reordering	**5.5%**	**5.5%**	63.8%	63.8%	93.5%	93.5%
M2-Urdu SLM-WOD-Tuned-With-Reordering	3.5%	3.5%	64.8%	64.8%	92.8%	92.8%
M2-Urdu SLM-WOD-Tuned-No-Reordering	3.5%	3.5%	64.8%	64.8%	92.8%	92.8%
M2-Urdu SLM+WLM-WOD-With-Reordering	5%	5%	**68.5%**	**68.5%**	**93.7%**	**93.7%**
M2-Urdu SLM+WLM-WOD -No-Reordering	5%	5%	**68.5%**	**68.5%**	**93.7%**	**93.7%**
M2-Urdu SLM+WLM-WOD -Tuned-With-Reordering	3%	3%	64.8%	64.8%	92.7%	92.7%
M2-Urdu SLM+WLM-WOD -Tuned-No-Reordering	3%	3%	64.8%	64.8%	92.7%	92.7%

Table 9: Test Set 2 results of Hindi–to–Urdu ST systems (character alignments

Abbreviation: SLM = sentence language model, WLM = word language model, WD = with diacritics, WOD = without diacritics.

The best results for the ST systems, developed from M2 are 68.5% and 5.5% at word-level and sentence-level, respectively, shown in bold in the lower grid of Table 9. In this case also, the best results at word-level and sentence-level are produced by different ST systems.

Figure 4 shows a sample Hindi source text from Test set 2 of Hindi origin.

भारतीय सांस्कृतिक परंपराएँ कपिला वात्स्यायन कलाओं के क्षेत्र में सृजनात्मक कार्य प्रश्न बहन जी , आप का विद्याध्ययन प्रतिभासूचक रहा है और उस के बाद भारत सरकार के संस्कृतिविभाग के अध्यक्ष के नाते भी आप का कार्य उच्चकोटि का रहा है ;
इस पद पर कार्य करते हुए आप पर भारत के अन्तर्राष्ट्रीय सांस्कृतिक सम्बन्धों और भारत के भीतर सांस्कृतिक नीति के निर्माण का दायित्व रहा है , इस क्षेत्र में ऐसी भिन्नभिन्न चीज़ें आती हैं जैसे संग्रहालय , पुरातत्व , पुरालेख , ग्रंथालय और कलाएँ ; केन्द्रीय स्तर पर भी और राज्य स्तर पर भी ।
आप का सरकारी कार्य तो भारत और विदेशों में सुविदित रहा है पर भारत की प्रदर्शनकारी और सुघट्य प्लास्टिक कलाओं के वर्गीकरण और व्याख्या करने के क्षेत्र में आप के सृजनात्मक योगदान के बारे में कम से कम औसत स्तर के शिक्षित सामान्य व्यक्ति को कुछ अधिक जानकारी नहीं है ।
क्या आप हमारे पाठकों के लिए भारतीय कलाओं और सौन्दर्यशास्त्र के क्षेत्र में किये गये अपने सृजनात्मक और अन्वेषणात्मक कार्य का संक्षिप्त विवरण देने की कृपा करें गी ?

Figure 4: A sample Hindi input text for Hindi–to–Urdu transliteration

Table 10 shows the Urdu output of the ST systems M1-Urdu SLM+WLM-WD-No-Reordering and M1-Urdu SLM-WD-No-Reordering that produced the best results at word-level and sentence-level, respectively.

Urdu reference without diacritics	Processed Urdu output of M1-Urdu SLM+WLM-WD-No-Reordering
بھارتیہ سانسکرتک پرنپراءیں کپلا واتسیاین کلاءوں کے کشیتر میں سرجناتمک کاریہ پرشن بہن جی ، آپ کا ودیادھیین پرتبھاسوچک رہا ہے اور اس کے بعد بھارت سرکار کے سنسکرتوبھاگ کے ادھیکش کے ناتے بھی آپ کا کاریہ اچکوٹی کا رہا ہے ؛ اس پد پر کاریہ کرتے ہوءے آپ پر بھارت کے انتراشٹریہ سانسکرتک سمبندھوں اور بھارت کے بھیتر سانسکرتک نیتی کے نرمان کا دایتو رہا ہے ، اس کشیتر میں ایسی بھنبھن چیزیں آتی ہیں جیسے سنگرہالیہ ، پراتتو ، پرالیکھ ، گرنتھالیہ اور کلاءیں ؛ کیندریہ سطر پر بھی اور راجیہ سطر پر بھی - آپ کا سرکاری کاریہ تو بھارت اور ودیشوں میں سودت رہا ہے پر بھارت کی پردرشنکاری اور سگھٹیہ پلاسٹک کلاءوں کے ورگیکرن اور ویاکھیا کرنے کے کشیتر میں آپ کے سرجناتمک یوگدان کے بارے میں کم سے کم اوسط سطر کے شکشت سامانیہ ویکتی کو کچھ ادھک جانکاری نہیں ہے - کیا آپ ہمارے پاٹھکوں کے لیے بھارتیہ کلاءوں اور سوندریشاستر کے کشیتر میں کیے گئے اپنے سرجناتمک اور انویشناتمک کاریہ کا سنکشپت وورن دینے کی کرپا کریں گی ؟	بھارتیہی سانسکرتک پرنپرہیں کپلا واتسیاین کلاوں کی کشیتر میں سرجناتمک کاریہ پرشن بہن جی ، آپ کا ویدیادھیین پرتیبھاسوچکا رہا ہے اور اس کی باد بھارت سرکار کی سنسکرتیوبھاگ کی ادھیکش کی ناتی بھی آپ کا کاریہ اچکوٹی کا رہا ہے ؛ اس پد پر کاریہ کرتی ہوای آپ پر بھارت کی انترراشٹریی سانسکرتک سمبندھوں اور بھارت کی بھیتر سانسکرتک نیتی کی نرمان کا داییتو رہا ہے ، اس کشیتر میں ایسی بھنبھن چیزیں آتی ہیں جیسی سنگرہالی ، پراتتو ، پرالیکھ ، گرنتھالی اور کلاءیں ؛ کیندریہ ستر پر بھی اور راجی ستر پر بھی - آپ کا سرکاری کاریہ تو بھارت اور ویدیشوں میں سویدت رہا ہے پر بھارت کی پردرشنکاری اور سگھٹی پلاسٹک کلاوں کی ورگیکرن اور ویاکھیا کرنی کی کشیتر میں آپ کی سرجناتمک یوگدان کی باری میں کم سی کم اوست ستر کی شکشت سامانی ویکتی کو کچھ ادھک جانکاری نہیں ہے - کیا آپ ہماری پاٹکوں کی لی بھارتیہی کلاوں اور سوندریشاسترہ کی کشیتر میں کیے گیے اپنی سرجناتمک اور انویشناتمک کاریہ کا سنکشپتہ ویورنہ دینی کی کرپا کریں گی ؟

Urdu reference without diacritics	Processed Urdu output of M1-Urdu SLM-WD-No-Reordering
بھارتیہ سانسکرتک پرنپراءیں کپلا واتسیاین کلاءوں کے کشیتر میں سرجناتمک کاریہ پرشن بہن جی ، آپ کا ودیادھیین پرتبھاسوچک رہا ہے اور اس کے بعد بھارت سرکار کے سنسکرتوبھاگ کے ادھیکش کے ناتے بھی آپ کا کاریہ اچکوٹی کا رہا ہے ؛ اس پد پر کاریہ کرتے ہوءے آپ پر بھارت کے انتراشٹریہ سانسکرتک سمبندھوں اور بھارت کے بھیتر سانسکرتک نیتی کے نرمان کا دایتو رہا ہے ، اس کشیتر میں ایسی بھنبھن چیزیں آتی ہیں جیسے سنگرہالیہ ، پراتتو ، پرالیکھ ، گرنتھالیہ اور کلاءیں ؛ کیندریہ سطر پر بھی اور راجیہ سطر پر بھی - آپ کا سرکاری کاریہ تو بھارت اور ودیشوں میں سودت رہا ہے پر بھارت کی پردرشنکاری اور سگھٹیہ پلاسٹک کلاءوں کے ورگیکرن اور ویاکھیا کرنے کے کشیتر میں آپ کے سرجناتمک یوگدان کے بارے میں کم سے کم اوسط سطر کے شکشت سامانیہ ویکتی کو کچھ ادھک جانکاری نہیں ہے - کیا آپ ہمارے پاٹھکوں کے لیے بھارتیہ کلاءوں اور سوندریشاستر کے کشیتر میں کیے گئے اپنے سرجناتمک اور انویشناتمک کاریہ کا سنکشپت وورن دینے کی کرپا کریں گی ؟	بھارتیہی سنسکرتیک پرنپرہیں کپیلا واتسیاین کلاوں کی کھیتر میں سرجناتمک کاریہ پرشن بہن جی ، آپ کا ویدیادھیین پرطبھاسوچکا رہا ہی اور اس کی باد بھارت سرکار کی سنسکرتیوبھاگا کی ادھیکس کی ناتی بھی آپ کا کاریہ اچکوٹی کا رہا ہی ؛ اس پد پر کاریہ کرتی ہوای آپ پر بھارت کی انترراشٹریے سنسکرتیک سمبندھوں اور بھارت کی بھیتر سنسکرتیک نیتی کی نرمان کا داییتو رہا ہی ، اس کھیتر میں ایسی بھینابھینین چیزیں آتی ہیں جیسے سنگرہالی ، پراتتو ، پرالیکھ ، گرنتھالی اور کلایں ؛ کیندریہ سر پر بھی اور راجی سر پر بھی - آپ کا سرکاری کاریہ تو بھارت اور ویدیشوں میں سویدیت رہا ہی پر بھارت کی پردرشنکاری اور سگھٹی پلاسٹک کلاوں کی ورگھیکرن اور ویاکھایا کرنے کی کھیتر میں آپ کی سرجناتمک یوگدان کی بھاری میں کم سی کم اوست سر کی شکسیت سامانی ویکتی کو کچھ ادھیک جانکاری نہیں ہی - کیا آپ ہماری پاٹکوں کی لی بھارتیہی کلاوں اور سوندریشاستر کی کھیتر میں کہیے گیے اپنے سرجناتمک اور انوےشناتمک کاریہ کا سنکششت ویوران دینو کی کرپا کریں گی ؟

Table 10: Sample Hindi–to–Urdu outputs with for the best ST systems for model M1

On average, there are 9.4 and 16 errors per sentence in the Urdu outputs of the ST systems M1-Urdu SLM+WLM-WD-No-Reordering and M1-Urdu SLM-WD-No-Reordering. In terms of usability of the output text, these outputs are not usable and require a huge amount of effort for post-editing. Therefore, these SMT systems would be ranked quite low by a user. From here onward, we will not give all results like we did in Table 9, but report only the results of particular interest.

For Test Set 3, the best results produced by the ST systems for models M1 and M2 are shown in Table 11.

SMT Model	Sentence Accuracy		Word accuracy		Character accuracy	
	default output	processed output	default output	processed output	default output	processed output
M1	0.9%	**4%**	57.3%	**71.1%**	90.6%	93.3%

Table 11: Test Set 3 results of Hindi–to–Urdu ST systems (character alignments)

For Test Set 2 and 3, the best results produced by the ST systems for models M3 and M4 are given in Table 12.

HU Test Set 2

SMT Model	Sentence accuracy		Word accuracy	
	default output	processed output	default output	processed output
M3	1%	**5.5%**	53.4%	**66.6%**
M4	**5.5%**	**5.5%**	65.3%	65.3%
M4	**5.5%**	**5.5%**	66.2%	66.2%
M4	**5.5%**	**5.5%**	69.5%	69.5%
M4	**5.5%**	**5.5%**	**69.7%**	**69.7%**

HU Test Set 3

SMT Model	Sentence Accuracy		Word accuracy	
	default output	processed output	default output	processed output
M3	0.9%	**4.9%**	58.0%	69.3%
M4	3.5%	3.5%	**68.0%**	**68.0%**
M4	3.5%	3.5%	**68.0%**	**68.0%**

Table 12: Test 2 and 3 results of Hindi–to–Urdu ST systems (cluster alignments)

For Test Set 1, the best results are 78.4% and 79.7% for the default and the processed Urdu output by the ST systems M4-Urdu SLM+WLM-WOD-Tuned-No-Reordering and M3-Urdu SLM+WLM-WD-Tuned-No-Reordering respectively. Test Set 1 consists of a word list, so there is no meaning of sentence-level results here. For Test Set 1, the best results are 78.3% and 80.2% for the default and the processed Urdu output by the ST systems M4-Urdu SLM+WLM-WOD-Tuned-No-Reordering and M3-Urdu SLM+WLM-WD-Tuned-No-Reordering respectively.

The ST systems developed from Urdu – Hindi parallel data without diacritics in the Urdu data are performing well compared to the systems developed from data that contains diacritical marks, because the removal of diacritical marks reduces the complexity of the transliteration problem.

5.3.2 Urdu–to–Hind transliteration results

Table 13 and Table 14 shows the best results of Urdu–to–Hindi transliteration of our ST systems for models M5 and M6 for HU Test Set 2 and 3 respectively.

HU Test Set 2

SMT Model	Sentence Accuracy		Word accuracy	
	with diacritics	without diacritics	with diacritics	without diacritics
M5	**5.5%**	2%	**72.2%**	57.9%
M5	**5.5%**	2%	**72.2%**	57.9%
M6	0.5%	5%	50.1%	**77.0%**
M6	0.5%	5%	50.1%	**77.0%**

Table 13: Test Set 2 best results for Urdu–to–Hindi ST systems (character alignments)

Urdu references with and without diacritics of Table 10 are our sample Urdu inputs for Urdu–to–Hindi transliteration. Table 15 shows the Hindi output for the sample Urdu input text with diacritics of the ST system M5-Hindi SLM+WLM-Tuned-No-Reordering with its Hindi reference. On average, the Hindi output of Table 15 contains 10.8 errors per sentence. A real user of the system would rate this output very low or even totally unacceptable.

HU Test Set 3

SMT Model	Sentence Accuracy		Word accuracy	
	with diacritics	without diacritics	with diacritics	without diacritics
M5	5.3%	0.4%	**77.8%**	57.9%
M5	5.3%	0.4%	**77.8%**	57.9%
M6	0%	0.4%	44.8%	**60.1%**
M6	0%	0.4%	44.8%	**60.1%**

Table 14: Test Set 3 best results for Urdu–to–Hindi ST systems (character alignments)

Urdu references with and without diacritics of Table 10 are our sample Urdu inputs for Urdu–to–Hindi transliteration. Table 15 shows the Hindi output for the sample Urdu input text with diacritics of the ST system M5-Hindi SLM+WLM-Tuned-No-Reordering with its Hindi reference. On average, the Hindi output of Table 15 contains 10.8 errors per sentence. A real user of the system would rate this output very low or even totally unacceptable.

Table 16 shows the Hindi output of the ST system M6-Hindi SLM+WLM-No-Reordering for the sample Urdu input without diacritics. The Hindi output of Table 16 also contains 10.8 errors per sentence.

Hindi reference	Hindi output from the Urdu text with diacritics M5-Hindi SLM+WLM-Tuned-No-Reordering
भारतीय सांस्कृतिक परंपराएँ	भारतीय सांस◌ंकृतिक परंपराईं
कपिला वात्स्यायन कलाओं के	कपिला वात◌ंस◌ंयायन कलावं के
क्षेत्र में सृजनात्मक कार्य प्रश्न	क◌ं◌्षेत◌ंर में सरज्ञात◌ंमक
बहन जी , आप का विद्याध्ययन	कार◌ं◌्य प◌ंरष◌ंन बहन जी , आप
प्रतिभासूचक रहा है और उस के	का विद◌ंयाध◌ंयेन प◌ंरतिभासूचक
बाद भारत सरकार के	रहा है और उस के बअद भारत
संस्कृतिविभाग के अध्यक्ष के	सरकार के संस◌ंकृतिविभाग के
नाते भी आप का कार्य उच्चकोटि	अध◌ं◌ेक◌ंष के नाते भी आप का
का रहा है ;	कार◌ं◌्य उच्चकोटी का रहा है ;
इस पद पर कार्य करते हुए आप	इस पद पर कार◌ं◌्य करते हूए
पर भारत के अन्तर्राष्ट्रीय	आप पर भारत के
सांस्कृतिक सम्बन्धों और भारत	अन◌ंतर्राष◌ंट◌ंरीया सांस◌ंकृतिक
के भीतर सांस्कृतिक नीति के	सम◌ंबन◌ंधों और भारत के भीतर
निर्माण का दायित्व रहा है , इस	सांस◌ंकृतिक नीति के निर◌ंमान
क्षेत्र में ऐसी भिन्नभिन्न चीज़ें	का दायित◌ं◌ो रहा है , इस
आती हैं जैसे संग्रहालय , पुरातत्व	क◌ं◌्षेत◌ंर में ऐसी भिन्नभिन्न
, पुरालेख , ग्रंथालय और कलाएँ ;	चीज़ें आती हैं जैसे संग◌ं◌्राल्य ,
केन्द्रीय स्तर पर भी और राज्य	पुरातत◌ं◌ो , पुरालेख , ग◌ंरंथाल्य
स्तर पर भी ।	और कलाईं ;
आप का सरकारी कार्य तो भारत	केन◌ंद◌ंरीया स◌ंतर पर भी और

और विदेशों में सुविदित रहा है पर भारत की प्रदर्शनकारी और सुघट्य प्लास्टिक कलाओं के वर्गीकरण और व्याख्या करने के क्षेत्र में आप के सृजनात्मक योगदान के बारे में कम से कम औसत स्तर के शिक्षित सामान्य व्यक्ति को कुछ अधिक जानकारी नहीं है। क्या आप हमारे पाठकों के लिए भारतीय कलाओं और सौन्दर्यशास्त्र के क्षेत्र में किये गये अपने सृजनात्मक और अन्वेषणात्मक कार्य का संक्षिप्त विवरण देने की कृपा करें गी ?	राज◌ं◌्य स◌ंतर पर भी । आप का सरकारी कार◌ं◌्य तो भारत और विदेशों में सुविदित रहा है पर भारत की प◌ंरदर◌ंशंकारी और सुघट◌ं◌्य प◌ंलास◌ंटिक कलावं के वर◌ंगीकरण और व◌ंयाख◌ंया करने के क◌ं◌्षेत◌ंर में आप के सरज्ञात◌ंमक योगदान के बारे में कम से कम औसत स◌ंतर के षिक◌ंषित सामान◌ं◌्य व◌ं◌ेक◌ंती को कुछ अधिक जानकारी नहीं है । क◌ंया आप हमारे पाठकों के लिये भारतीय कलावं और सौन◌ंदर◌ं◌ेषास◌ंत◌ंर के क◌ं◌्षेत◌ंर में किये ग◌ु◌े अपने सरज्ञात◌ंमक और अन◌ंवेशनात◌ंमक कार◌ं◌्य का सनक◌ंषिप◌ंत विवरन देने की कृपा करें गी ?

Table 15: A sample Hindi output with its reference from Urdu input with diacritics

Hindi reference	Hindi output from the Urdu text without diacritics M6-Hindi SLM+WLM-Tuned-No-Reordering
भारतीय सांस्कृतिक परंपराएँ कपिला वात्स्यायन कलाओं के क्षेत्र में सृजनात्मक कार्य प्रश्न बहन जी , आप का विद्याध्ययन प्रतिभासूचक रहा है और उस के बाद भारत सरकार के संस्कृतिविभाग के अध्यक्ष के नाते भी आप का कार्य उच्चकोटि का रहा है ; इस पद पर कार्य करते हुए आप पर भारत के अन्तर्राष्ट्रीय सांस्कृतिक सम्बन्धों और भारत के भीतर सांस्कृतिक नीति के निर्माण का दायित्व रहा है , इस क्षेत्र में ऐसी भिन्नभिन्न चीज़ें आती हैं जैसे संग्रहालय , पुरातत्व , पुरालेख , ग्रंथालय और कलाएँ ; केन्द्रीय स्तर पर भी और राज्य स्तर पर भी । आप का सरकारी कार्य तो भारत और विदेशों में सुविदित रहा है पर भारत की प्रदर्शनकारी और सुघट्य प्लास्टिक कलाओं के वर्गीकरण और व्याख्या करने के क्षेत्र में आप के सृजनात्मक योगदान के बारे में कम से कम औसत स्तर के शिक्षित सामान्य व्यक्ति को कुछ अधिक जानकारी नहीं है । क्या आप हमारे पाठकों के लिए भारतीय कलाओं और सौन्दर्यशास्त्र के क्षेत्र में किये गये अपने सृजनात्मक और अन्वेषणात्मक कार्य का संक्षिप्त विवरण देने की कृपा करें गी ?	भारतीय सांस◌ंकृतिक परंपराईं कपिला वात◌ंस◌ंयायन कलावं के क◌ं◌्षेत◌ंर में सरज्ञात◌ंमक कार◌ं◌्य प◌ंरष◌ंन बहन जी , आप का विद◌ंयाध◌ंयेन प◌ंरतिभासूचक रहा है और उस के बअद भारत सरकार के संस◌ंकृतिविभाग के अध◌ं◌ेक◌ंष के नाते भी आप का कार◌ं◌्य उच्चकोटी का रहा है ; इस पद पर कार◌ं◌्य करते हूए आप पर भारत के अन◌ंतर्राष◌ंट◌ंरीया सांस◌ंकृतिक सम◌ंबन◌ंधों और भारत के भीतर सांस◌ंकृतिक नीति के निर◌ंमान का दायित◌ं◌ो रहा है , इस क◌ं◌्षेत◌ंर में ऐसी भिन्नभिन्न चीज़ें आती हैं जैसे संग◌ं◌्राल्य , पुरातत◌ं◌ो , पुरालेख , ग◌ंरंथाल्य और कलाईं ; केन◌ंद◌ंरीया स◌ंतर पर भी और राज◌ं◌्य स◌ंतर पर भी । आप का सरकारी कार◌ं◌्य तो भारत और विदेशों में सुविदित रहा है पर भारत की प◌ंरदर◌ंशंकारी और सुघट◌ं◌्य प◌ंलास◌ंटिक कलावं के वर◌ंगीकरण और व◌ंयाख◌ंया करने के क◌ं◌्षेत◌ंर में आप के सरज्ञात◌ंमक योगदान के बारे में कम से कम औसत स◌ंतर के षिक◌ंषित सामान◌ं◌्य व◌ं◌ेक◌ंती को कुछ अधिक जानकारी नहीं है । क◌ंया आप हमारे पाठकों के लिये भारतीय कलावं और सौन◌ंदर◌ं◌ेषास◌ंत◌ंर के क◌ं◌्षेत◌ंर में किये ग◌ु◌े अपने सरज्ञात◌ंमक और अन◌ंवेशनात◌ंमक कार◌ं◌्य का सनक◌ंषिप◌ंत विवरन देने की कृपा करें गी ?

Table 16: A sample Hindi output with its reference from Urdu input without diacritics

In general, the sentence-level accuracy of an ST system is always between 5% to 10%. The reason behind this very low accuracy might be the training data. In our case, the training data is an Urdu – Hindi parallel lexicon and not a parallel corpus (a usual case for a classical SMT system). Unfortunately, we do not have any Hindi-Urdu parallel corpus to test our hypothesis that the accuracy of Hindi-Urdu transliteration can be improved by training the ST models with Hindi-Urdu parallel corpus instead of using a Hindi-Urdu parallel lexicon.

6 Conclusion

A mere transliteration between Urdu and Hindi can serve the purpose of translation between Urdu and Hindi. Urdu and Hindi are linguistically the same or almost the same languages because of their common grammatical structure, morphology and roughly 60 to 70% common vocabulary. Thus Urdu Hindi transliteration is very important for more than 1,000 million people on the globe.

In this paper we have reported our experiments on Urdu↔Hindi transliteration using Statistical Machine Translation (SMT) techniques and an Urdu – Hindi parallel lexical resource. We have performed total 576 experiments and have reported results of significant interest. From Hindi–to–Urdu transliteration, we have achieved the maximum word-level accuracy of 71.5%. From Urdu–to–Hindi transliteration, the maximum word-level accuracy is 77.8% when the input Urdu text contains all necessary diacritical marks and 77% when the input Urdu text does not contain all necessary diacritical marks. At character-level, transliteration accuracy is more than 90% in both directions. At the sentence-level, the accuracy of an ST system is always between 5% to 10%. This is a very low in terms of readability and usability of a transliterated text. These results can be improved by building an Urdu Hindi parallel corpus and by building context sensitive transliteration models. We will show in future that a better high quality Urdu – Hindi transliteration system can be built by combining non-deterministic finite-state transliteration models and finite-state language models.

Acknowledgments

We are thankful to Mr. James Nye, project director of Digital South Asia Library (DSAL), University of Chicago for sharing their digital data of "A dictionary of Urdu, classical Hindi and English" with us.

References

AbdulJaleel, Nasreen and Larkey, L. S. 2003. Statistical Transliteration for English-Arabic Cross Language Information Retrieval. *12th international Conference on information and Knowledge Management (CIKM 03)*, pp. 139-46. New Orleans: ACM.

Al-Onaizan, Yaser and Knight, Kevin. 2002. Machine Transliteration of Names in Arabic Text. *Workshop on Computational Approaches To Semitic Languages, the 40th Annual Meeting of the ACL*, pp. 1-13. Philadelphia, Pennsylvania: ACL.

Al-Onaizan, Yaser and Papineni, Kishore. 2006. Distortion Models for Statistical Machine Translation. *21st International Conference on Computational Linguistics (COLING) and 44th Annual Meeting of the ACL*, pp. 529–36. Sydney, Australia.

Brown, Peter F., Cocke, John, Pietra, Stephen A. Della, Pietra, Vincent J. Della, Jelinek, Fredrick, Lafferty, John D., Mercer, Robert L. and Roossin, Paul S. 1990. A Statistical Approach to Machine Translation. *Computational Linguistics* 16(2): 79-85.

Brown, Peter F., Pietra, Stephen A. Della, Pietra, Vincent J. Della and Mercer, Robert L. 1993. The Mathematics of Statistical Machine Translation: parameter estimation. *Computational Linguistics* 19(2): 263-312.

Durrani, Nadir, Sajjad, Hassan, Fraser, Alexander and Schmid, Helmut. 2010. Hindi-to-Urdu Machine Translation Through Transliteration. *the 48th Annual Meeting of the Association for Computational Linguistics*, pp. 465–74. Uppsala, Sweden.

Ekbal, Asif, Naskar, Sudip Kumar and Bandyopadhyay, Sivaji. 2006. A Modified Joint Source-channel Model for Transliteration. *21st International Conference on Computational Linguistics (COLING) and the 44th Annual Meeting of the ACL*, pp. 191-98. Sydney: ACL & ICCL.

Finch, Andrew and Sumita, Eiichiro. 2009. Transliteration by Bidirectional Statistical Machine Translation. *workshop on Named Entities (NEWS-09), Joint Conference of the 47th Annual Meeting of the ACL and the 4th International Joint Conference on Natural Language Processing ACL/IJCNLP*, pp. 52-56. Singapore.

Fraser, Alexander and Marcu, Daniel. 2007. Measuring Word Alignment Quality for Statistical Machine Translation. *Computational Linguistics* 33(3): 293-303.

Huang, Fei. 2009. Confidence Measure for Word Alignment. *Joint Conference the 47th Annual Meeting of the ACL and the 4th IJCNLP*, pp. 932-40. Singapore.

Hussain, Sarmad. 2004. Letter-to-Sound Conversion for Urdu Text-to-Speech System. *Workshop on Computational Approaches to Arabic Scriptbased Languages, International Conference on Computational Linguistics (COLING)*, pp. 74-79. Geneva: ICCL.

Khan, Abdul Jamil. 2006. *Urdu/Hindi: an artificial divide*. New York: Algora Publishing.

Kirschenbaum, Amit and Wintner, Shuly. 2009. Lightly Supervised Transliteration for Machine Translation. *12th Conference of the European Chapter of the ACL*, pp. 433-41. Athens: ACL.

Knight, Kevin and Graehl, Jonathan. 1997. Machine Transliteration. *8th Conference of EACL*, pp. 128-35. Madrid: ACL.

Koehn, Philipp. 2010. *Statistiacal Machine Translation*. Cambridge University Press.

Koehn, Philipp, Hoang, Hieu, Birch, Alexandra, Callison-Burch, Chris, Federico, Marcello, Bertoldi, Nicola, Cowan, Brooke, Shen, Wade, Moran, Christine, Zens, Richard, Dyer, Chris, Bojar, Ondřej, Constantin, Alexandra and Herbst, Evan. 2007. Moses: open source toolkit for Statistical Machine Translation. *47th Association for Computational Linguistics 2007 Demo and Poster Sessions*, pp. 177-80. Prague.

Koehn, Philipp, Och, Franz Josef and Marcu, Daniel. 2003. Statistical Phrase-Based Translation. *Human Language Technology (HLT), NAACL-2003*, pp. 48-54. Edmonton, Canada.

Kumar, Shankar, Och, Franz and Macherey, Wolfgang. 2007. Improving Word Alignment with Bridge Languages. *Joint Conference on Empirical Methods in Natural Language Processing and Computational Natural Language Learning*, pp. 42-50.

Lee, J. S. and Choi., K. S. 1998. English to Korean Statistical Transliteration for Information Retrieval. *Computer Processing of Oriental languages* 12(1): 17-37.

Lewis, M. Paul. 2009. Ethnologue: Languages of the World. In M. P. Lewis (ed.). Dallas: SIL International.

Li, Haizhou, Zhang, Min and Su, Jian. 2004. A Joint Source-channel Model for Machine Transliteration. *42nd Annual Meeting on ACL*, Barcelona: ACL.

Lopez, Adam. 2008. Statistical Machine Translation. *ACM Computing Surveys* 40(3).

Malik, M. G. Abbas, Besacier, Laurent, Boitet, Christian and Bhattacharyya, Pushpak. 2009. A Hybrid Model for Urdu Hindi Transliteration. *Joint conference of the 47th Annual Meeting of the Association of Computational Linguistics and the 4th International Joint Conference on Natural Language Processing of the Asian Federation of NLP ACL/IJCNLP Workshop on Named Entities (NEWS-09)*, pp. 177–85. Singapore.

Malik, M. G. Abbas, Boitet, Christian and Bhattacharyya, Pushpak. 2008. Hindi Urdu Machine Transliteration using Finite-state Transducers. *22nd International Conference on Computational Linguistics (COLING)*, pp. 537-44. Manchester: ICCL.

Nabende, Peter. 2009. Transliteration System using pair HMM with Weighted FSTs. *Joint conference of the 47th Annual Meeting of the Association of Computational Linguistics and the 4th International Joint Conference on Natural Language Processing of the Asian Federation of NLP ACL/IJCNLP Workshop on Named Entities (NEWS-09)*, pp. 100–03. Singapore: IJCNLP/ACL.

Och, Franz Josef and Ney, Hermann. 2003. A Systematic Comparison of Various Statistical Alignment Models. *Computational Linguistics* 29(1): 19-51.

Och, Franz Josef and Ney, Hermann. 2004. The Alignment Template Approach to Statistical Machine Translation. *Computational Linguistics* 30(4): 417-49.

Platts, John T. 1884. A Dictionary of Urdu, Classical Hindi and Englsih. London: W. H. Allen & Co.

Platts, John T. 1909. *A Grammar of the Hindustani or Urdu Language*. Crosby Lockwood and Son.

Rabinder, Lawrence R. 1989. A tutorial on Hidden Markon Models and selected applications in speech recognition. *IEEE*, pp. 257-85.

Rabiner, L. and Juang, B. H. 1986. An Introduction to Hidden Markov Models. *IEEE ASSP Magazine* 3(1): 4-16.

Rahman, T. 2004. Language Policy and Localization in Pakistan: Proposal for a Paradigmatic Shift. *Crossing the Digital Divide, SCALLA Conference on Computational Linguistics*, Katmandu.

Rai, Alok. 2000. *Hindi Nationalism*. New Delhi: Orient Longman Private Limited.

Stall, B. and Knight, K. 1998. Translating Names and Technical Terms in Arabic Text. *Workshop on Computational Approaches to Semitic Languages, COLING/ACL*, pp. 34-41. Montreal.

Zens, Richard and Ney, Hermann. 2003. A Comparative Study on Reordering Constraints in Statistical Machine Translation. *41st Annual Meeting on Association for Computational Linguistics*, pp. 144-51. Sapporo, Japan.

Zia, Khaver. 1999. Standard Code Table for Urdu. *4th Symposium on Multilingual Information Processing (MLIT-4)*, Yangon: CICC.

Urdu Spell Checking: Reverse Edit Distance Approach

Saadat Iqbal, Waqas Anwar, Usama Ijaz Bajwa, Zobia Rehman
COMSATS Institute of Information Technology, Abbottabad, Pakistan
{saadat,waqas,usama,zobiarehman}ciit.net.pkemail@domain

Abstract

Spelling of words of a language are standardized by language authorities or consortiums and available in dictionaries or lexicons. For instance, "produkt" does not belong to English dictionary. Similarly "درميان" is a correctly spelled word, while "درميانر " is a non-word in Urdu. Electronic representation of text is commonly used in today's computing environment. The rich resourced languages like English have many applications with added tools. On the other hand, application development is in its infancy for less resourced language like Urdu. Spelling plays a vital role while humans write text electronically in computers. It is oblivious that terabytes of text is added in form of corpus or otherwise that is required to be spell checked, which is practically impossible to be done manually. In this work, various techniques for spellchecking have been studied and analyzed. All of them separately or a combination thereof can be used for the process of spell checking. Edit Distance technique has been widely used in spell checkers of various language, and a variation of this technique i.e. Reverse Edit Distance technique selected for suggesting correct words for nonwords. For Urdu, candidates are found by making 86n+41 comparisons for an 'n character' length Urdu word.

1 Introduction

Usage of computers became an essential component in human lives. In today's computing environment, text processors, search engines, short messaging services, chatting applications, and many more are widely used. Google auto complete feature starts giving options; For instance when "morp" is typed options like: morphine, morphology, morphine drug, and morphological choices appear. On the other hand the user does not know the exact spelling, Google will make a search based on closed matched words and will display the message as well. All this happens in a fraction of second. This reveals that Google and other applications are using spell error detections and correction algorithms which are implemented in applications for user facilitation. Terabytes of text added to the internet resource daily is required to be spellchecked. A single book requires multilevel readers for spell checking and correction, if performed manually. Thus automated spell checkers and correctors are required.

Spell checking is process of matching a given word with alphabetically ordered words in a dictionary or lexicon. For instance, in Urdu, a given word شابين is compared with words in Urdu lexicon, if we get a match then the word is considered to be correctly spelled. On the other hand if we compare شاحين with words in lexicon, if we do not get a match then the word is considered to be misspelled. However it is worth mentioning here that the automated spell checking process is reasonably complex in case of Urdu as compare to English. The complex process of spell checking in Urdu is due to its morphologically richness, word space problem, and scarcely available electronic resources.

The spell checking process is a pre-requisite for language processing systems, e.g. Grammar checker, Part of speech (PoS) tagging, Information extraction, Machine translation, etc. The input to above mentioned language process systems must be correctly spelled, and the text must be passed through a dependent spell checker.

Section 2 narrates about the challenges exists about spell checking in Urdu, Linguist study is narrated in section 3, section 4 discusses proposed technique for Urdu spell checking, the review of review of reverse edit distance algortithms and discussion are presented in section 5, and section 6 is for conclusion.

2 Challenges of Urdu Spell Checking

Tokenization in Urdu, Diction problem, Loan Words, Morphological nature, Grammatical words and Initial letter Capitalization are some of the challenges that makes the Urdu Spell checking complex. Tokenization is process of to break text at word level.

2.1 Word Separator – space character

In English text, words are separated by spaces characters, as tokens (Sara Stymne 2011). To separate words in Urdu, spaces are not used after every word as in case of English language. The natives of Urdu language separate the words from each other by cognitive knowledge of the language while reading or writing text. For instance, in the following example same sentence is written in three variation of space usage:
Space is only used after a word that ends with joiner letter. ہم بازارمیں کھیل رہے تھے- [We were playing in the bazaar]. Space is not used at all after any of the word that ends with joiner letter.ہمبازارمینکھیلرہےتھے- Space is used after each word. ہم بازارمیں کھیل ر ہے تھے-

2.2 Morphological Nature

In contrast to languages like English, Urdu language bends toward agglutinative languages due to its complex morphological nature. The languages like Turkish and Finnish are agglutinative languages as multiple words generates from a single word by affixation, derivational, and inflectional suffixes. From the Turkish word "uggar" (means civilized) a word "uggarlastiramayabileceklerimizdenmissinizcesine" is derived (Kemal Oflazer and Cemaleddin 1994). "Heater", "heated", "heats" are the word forms that are inflected from the root word "heat". Urdu is morphological rich language and multiple words are inflected from a root word. The following are few inflected words that are inflected from the root word of Urdu بول (speak).

تو بول
تم بولو
تم بولنا
آپ بولیں
آپ بولیئے
آپ بولتے
آپ بولو

2.3 Diction Problem

Diction problem is defined as using choice of words from a set of word which has same meanings. The Urdu language is considered to be computationally complex due to its diction problem as well. Example words in Urdu that are different in spelling but having same meanings are: (تکیا، تکیہ)

2.4 Loan Words

The native speakers of the Urdu language take advantage of **loan words** from other languages like English. Engine: (انجن), O-Level (O-لیول کے طلباء). Paragraph (پیراگراف)

2.5 Initial letter Capitalization

In English proper nouns, start of sentences can be recognized with the words with letter capitalized. For instance,

- The world is shrinking .... [initial letter of "The" is capitalized at the beginning of sentence]
- The delegation will meet Abu Bakar at Islamabad .... [initial letter of proper nouns "Abu Bakar" and "Islamabad" are capitalized.

وفد ابوبکر سےاسلام اباد میں ملاقات کرے گا۔ [proper nouns starting with a normal character].

2.6 Grammatical Words

Grammatical words are prepositions, adverbs, conjunctions etc. they themselves have not a very clear meaning. However, these words are used to complete sentences and there meanings are expressed in dictionaries with the help of examples. For instance, for, with, the, of, etc. In Urdu the examples of grammatical words are, سے ، نے ، کا etc. *say, nay, kaa* respectively.

3 Literature Review

3.1 Historic perspective of Spell Checking

Wherever there is text processing, misspelled words come across, and these misspelled words are required to be detected and corrected. Thus research in spell detection and correction started in the period when text processing become common for computer users. In 1964, Fred J Damerau, articles (Fred J. Damerau 1964) explained fundamentals techniques for spelling detection and correction. According to Damerau, spell checking is a process of comparing an input index with a master list of acceptable terms, and rejects those word from the input which has no match in the master list. In tests conducted by Damerau, indicated that 80% of the spelling errors falls in single letter error, these errors are:
Substitution; a letter is wrongly substituted by another letter,

Insertion; a letter is wrongly inserted at some position,
Deletion; a letter is wrongly deleted from some position,
Transposition; two letters are wrongly transposed.
Few examples words that are taken from the test data of Damerau are given in a Table 1.

Error type	Correct word	Misspelled word
Substitution	Absorbent	Absorbant
Insertion	Commitment	Committment
Deletion	Governmentt	Government
Transposition	Wierd	Weird

Table 1: Extracts from Damerau Test data

In a test conducted by Damrau, a data of 964 spell errors was taken for conducting a test. The results are presented in Table 2.

	Substitution	Deletion	Transposition	Insertion	Multiple errors	Total
Correctly identified	549	143	23	97	0	812
Incorrectly identified	18	10	0	2	0	30
Not identified	0	0	0	0	122	122
Total	567	153	23	99	122	964

Table 2: Major error types for spelling errors

3.2 Spelling Error classification

Spelling errors are classified into two types, namely typographic errors and cognitive errors (Kyongho Min, William H. Wilson, Yoo-Jin Moon), (Tahira Naseem 2004). Typographic errors are those errors in which the person typing the text knows spelling, however mistype the word. For instance, a user intends to type "listen" but wrongly types "listyen". The additional adjacent key 'y' is pressed while the typist intended to type 't' in the word "listen". Thus, the "listyen" example pertains to insertion as explained by Damerau. In case of cognitive error, spelling of word is not known to the writer. Due to existence of homophone alphabet set in Urdu language, cognitive errors are found in the Urdu written text. For instance [ض, ذ]

For Urdu spelling errors trends, a study was conducted by (Tahira Naseem et al). The data for the study was taken from newspaper text, and students term papers. In English, [s, c] are phonetically equivalent, or termed as homophone alphabets; given in example [race, rase]. In case of Urdu text, there are several homophones characters sets. For instance [ذ، ز، ض]. Similarly، visually similar character also exists in Urdu text [د، ذ]. Their study exhibited the results illustrated in Table 3.

	Newspaper Text		
	Total errors	Visually Similar	Phonetically similar
Substitution	75	40	12
Deletion	42	4	5
Insertion	21	2	1
Transposition	12	3	0
Total	150	49	18

Table 3: Single Edit Distance Errors in Urdu

3.3 Spelling Error correction techniques

The spelling correction solution comprises of three phases:

- Detection of Spelling error
- Finding candidate word(s) for the misspelled words
- Order candidate according to match strength

The following are the techniques that are employed by various spell correction tools in many languages.

- Minimum Edit Distance technique
- Similarity Key technique
- Neural Networks technique

3.3.1 Minimum Edit Distance Technique

In 1965, the Minimum Edit Distance technique was given by Vladimir Levenshtein, to compute minimum edit distance or edit operation required to transform one string *str1* to another string *str2*. In this technique, a matrix is taken of dimension *m* x *n*, where *m*, and *n* represents the length of two strings *str1*, and *str2*. One of the string say *str1*, is placed at the top row of matrix, and the *str2* is placed at leftmost column. On execution of Edit Distance algorithm, each cell of the matrix is filled with the difference of edit operations performed.

The Minimum Edit Distance algorithm measures distance between two strings. An *insertion* operation takes place, when a alphabet is inserted in a non-word sequence to make it correct word. Similarly, *deletion* operation takes place, when a alphabet is deleted from a non-word sequence to make it correct word, *substitution* operation takes place when a alphabet is substituted in a non-word sequence to make it correct word. If there are *w* number of words in a lexicon, the minimum edit distance algorithm performs *w* comparisons of a misspelled word with all w words in dictionary. To minimize the comparisons, reverse edit distance algorithm (Eric Brill and Robert C. Moore), (M. D. Kernighan, K. W. Church, and W. A. Gale 1990) is proposed. In modified algorithm only 53n + 25 words comparisons are performed, where n is length of misspelled English word.

3.3.2 Similarity Key Technique

This technique is based upon the key assignment to the words of a language. Words are composed of alphabet. In this technique a set of alphabet is taken based on sound similarity. It is to be noted that the key is not unique, and will be explained shortly. The following are the sets in Similarity Key technique.

Digit of Key	Alphabet
0	a,e,i,o,u,h,w,y
1	b,f,p,v
2	c,g,j,k,q,s,x,z
3	d,t
4	L
5	m, n
6	R

Table 4: Similarity keys for English Alphabets

In this technique, the key is calculated for a misspell word. Then the words from the lexicon that have the same key value are extracted for candidature of a correctly spelled word. The key are generated by keeping the first letter of the word followed by digits mapped from the Table 4. For instance the key t0140 is generated for the word *table*. The zero and are eliminated from the key. Similarly repetition of a character is collapsed. Thus in second step the key t0140 becomes t14 for the word *table*.

The Urdu character set is also composed of many homophones. A study has been conducted (Tahira Naseem 2004) on spelling mistakes of Urdu words in context to soundex.

The similar Urdu sounded letter are shown in Table 5, and Table 6 of soundex scheme 0-F, and 0-9 respectively.

code	Alphabet
0	س،ش، ص، ث
1	ت، ط، ٹ
2 ~ D	--------
E	ل
F	و

Table 5: Similar sounded letters – Urdu (Scheme 0 ~ F)

code	Alphabet
0	س،ش، ص، ث
1	ت، ط، ٹ
2 ~ 8	--------
9	ل

Table 6: Similar sounded letters – Urdu (Scheme 0 ~ 9)

3.3.3 Neural Networks Technique

Neural networks are used in environments where systems are trained on specific error patterns (O. Matan, C. J. C. Burges, Y. LeCun, and J. S. Denker 1992). Thus neural networks can be used for spell correction. The neural network is trained in for spell errors for a specific domain in which the spell correction system will be used. The back propagation method is commonly used in neural network training (V. J. Hodge and J. Austin 2003). The method comprised of three layers; the input, hidden, and output layer. The nodes from inner to output layer are connected through a link through hidden layer. In the training phase, weights are computed and assigned to the nodes from input layer to output layer. The weights represent the relation between the nodes.

4 Proposed Technique for Urdu Spell Checking - Reverse Edit Distance

It is obvious that q linear comparisons are required for a misspelled word with all words of lexicon containing q words. 70,000 words lexicon, requires 70,000 comparisons. Reverse edit distance technique is proposed (M. D. Kernighan, K. W. Church, and W. A. Gale 1990) in which permutation of edit distance one are generated and compared with lexicon words which are in alphabetic order. Urdu has 42 characters, and for a Urdu word of length n, a total of 86n + 41 strings are checked, which is far below than lexicon words q. The break-up is as under:

Insertions ofے ،ی .. ،ب ،ا at n+1 positions in a word. 42(n+1)

Deletion of one alphabet in turn from word. n

Substitution ofے ،ی ..... ،ب ،ا in turn at each position in word 42n

Transpositions of adjacent alphabets in word n-1

----------------------- ----------

Total comparisons 86n + 41

============== ========

The reverse edit distance technique can be employed for Urdu Spell system. The usage of this technique is selected due to its efficient approach.

Urdu misspelled word w = '**نهک**. '

Substitutes:

The first letter 'ن' of Urdu misspelled word نھک is substituted with ے، ی ..... ب، ا in turn resulting:

ےھک'----------, 'تھک', 'پھک', 'بھک', 'اھک'

Likewise, The second letter 'ھ' of misspelled word نھک is substituted with alphabet ے، ی ..... ب، ا in turn resulting: نےک---------، نمک----------، نتک، نپک، نبک، ناک

Likewise, The third, and fourth letter get substituted.

Inserts :

In next set of permutations, characters ے، ی ..... ب، ا are inserted in turn at position 1,2,3, and 4 of the misspelled word نھک.

ینھک، .... ,تنھک ,پنھک , بنھک ,انھک

Transposes

نکھ ,ھنک

Deletes

نھ,نک ، ھک

4.1 Dictionary lookup

Finite State Automata (FSA) are based on alphabets U of a language L. A string S, comprises of alphabet from U. If S belongs to U, then there will be a path from the initial state to the final state of the Finite state automata, else will declare mispelled word.
If a correct word that is not available in the lexicon would be required to be added while the spell checking application highlight as a misplelled word.

4.2 Edit Distance (Two operations)

Despite the fact that misspelled words are corrected by one edit operation. Thus it may happen that out of 86n + 41 permutations generated from an Urdu non-word may lead to zero match in the lexicon. Thus in our proposed work, edit distance is procedure is called again on all the permutation generated by the edit distance one operation. This drastically slows down the system as permutations (2nd cycle) for each of the permutation generated at edit distance 1 will be generated.

4.3 Candidate Generation

Candidates are selected upon the existence of any match of the permuted word in lexicon. In our example case two candidates are generated: *c* = ['نمک', 'نیک']

4.4 Reverse Edit Distance Efficiency

The Reverse Edit Distance algorithm is grossly better than the conventional Edit Distance algorithm. This can be explained with simple calculation on data.

Lexicon size (q) = 100,000 words
Misspelled word length (n) = 6 letters

	Edit Distance	**Reverse Edit Distance**
Comparisons	100,000	86n + 41 =86(6) + 41 = 557

Thus in this example the reverse edit distance performs 180 times better as compare to edit distance technique.

4.5 Methodology Digest

This work presents spell checking for Urdu non-words employing lexicon lookup. Spell checkers are not available in the Urdu text processors, and the most important among them is the widely used Urdu Word processor still lacking the spell checking and correcting feature.
The Levenshtein distance or most commonly minimum edit distance algorithm is used as a basic and acceptable technique for spell correction. In our work, the same algorithm has been selected for getting candidate words for an Urdu non-word.
The working model of the proposed system is kept simple, being the system is build on basic works, as very scarce resources are available on Urdu Language and specifically the Urdu spell checking and correction. A three step approach has been employed in the system: Lexicon lookup, candidates' generation, and ranking candidates.
The system uses an lexicon or corpus that contain the correctly spell words, and this corpus is referred by system for ensuring that the given word is misspelled word or otherwise If match of input word is found in underlying corpus then word is correctly spelled, and declared misplelled if not found. For misspelled word, the process of finding correctly spelled word candidate starts. At this step, the Levenshtein distance or most commonly minimum edit distance algorithm is used to get the candidates. Most of the errors are at distance one. Damerau has observed that 80% of the error lies at edit distance one, that the 80% of the misspelled words need one edit operation of substitution, insertion, deletion, and transposition. For generation of candidates, edit distance one, and edit distance two has been used. The union of results of both edit distance one and edit distance two is taken to produce a list of candidate words. In the third and last step, best probable correctly spelled word for the mis-

spelled word based on the frequency of candidates word exists in the underlying corpus. The methodology is explained in the illustration:

Misspelled word	Corpus	Candidate words	Top ranked word
ادر	Urdu corpus	ادا (34) اتر (23) اثر (2) صدر (40) اگر (12)	صدر get selected.

Table 7. Illustration explaining methodology

In the above illustration, for the misspelled Urdu word ادر we have taken few candidate words ادا، اتر، اثر، صدر ، اگر shown in the third column of Table 7 which are at edit distance one, that is one edit operation we can get these words from the misspelled word. Now to decide which of these candidate words is intended correct word that typist wanted to write cannot be flatly decided.

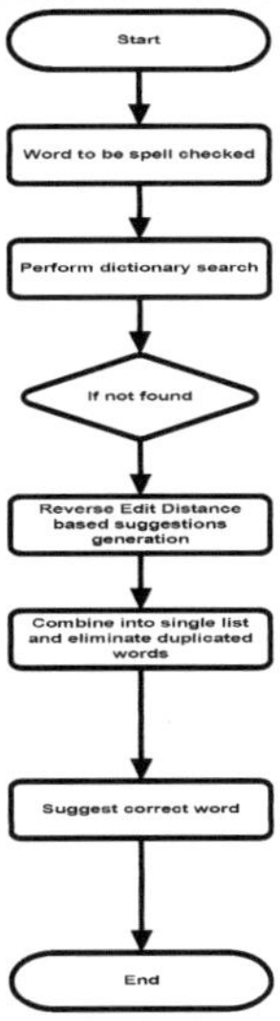

Figure 1. Flow chart depicting the process of spell checking and correction

5 Results and Discussions

5.1 Training Corpus

Two corpuses of 54,440 words, and 56,142 words [Center For Research In Urdu Language Processing] are taken that has been used as training lexicon. In subsequent work later, a comprehensive corpus will be taken for results. The training data is used for frequency count of the words. The frequency count is used for analysis of candidate words from a misspelled word. Let's take a simple corpus of 20 Urdu words to understand the training set concept:

ابتدائی نتائج ایک سو سال سے کچھ پہلے بتائے گئے تھے
مگر تازہترین نتائج پچھلے سال اور اس سال سے پہلے

In the work presented, small hypothetical data is taken to understand the concept. In future, with implemantation of algorithms, accuracy will be also bw calculated.

The frequency of these words is shown in the Table 8

الفاظ (Words)	تعداد (Frequency)
ابتدائی	1
نتائج	2
ایک	1
سال	3
سو	1
سے	2
کچھ	2
پہلے	1
بتائے	1
گئے	1
تھے	1
مگر	1
تازہترین	1
پچھلے	1
اور	1
اس	1

Table 8. Frequency – Mini training set data

Now taking misspelled word سق, let the spell correction system generate two candidates; the word سو [frequency count = 1], and the word سے [frequency count = 2]. Based on frequency, suggested word is calculated which comes to be سے for the misspelled word سق

Taking another example of few misspelled words and executing our algorithm on a training set corpus of 54,400 words. We would see abstract behavior of algorithm and make a little discussion on the result generated. The following nonwords are provided to the system for generation of candidate words, there after highlighting one word.

5.2 Urdu Non-words example

استعال کطی جاتپی تی مییں جشس کشتی جشگہ ایشک دوسشری قشسم کشے فلشٹر

Test word –i استعال

Candidate word(s) استعال

Suggested word استعال

================================

Test word- ii کطی

Candidate word(s) کری کئی کسی

Suggested word کسی

====================================

Test word - iii جاتپی

Candidate word(s) جاتی ساتھی

Suggested word جاتی

====================================

Test word –iv مییں

Candidate word(s) میں ملیں نہیں

Suggested word میں

====================================

Test word-v جشس

Candidate word(s) باس جس جدا

Suggested word جس

====================================

Test word - vi کششی

Candidate word(s) کسری کرتی

Suggested word کرتی

====================================

Test word-vii جشگہ

Candidate word(s) جگہ جبکہ

Suggested word جبکہ

====================================

Test word-viii کشے

Candidate word(s) کتے کئے کرے

Suggested word کرے

====================================

Test word-ix فلشٹر

Candidate word(s) فوسٹر فلٹر

Suggested word فلٹر

====================================

In the above example, we have taken 09 non-words of Urdu and pass through the reverse edit distance algorithm. Candidate words in the range of one to three words are generated for each of the non word. These are words are at edit distance of one or two from the corresponding non-word. The candidate words are generated by insertions, deletion, substitution, or transposition operations.

5.3 Correct word suggestion

In the corpus the c(جاتی) = 22, and c(ساتھی) = 5, Thus c(جاتی) > c(ساتھی) thus the word جاتی is suggested as the top ranked word for the misspelled word *w* = جاتپی

Insertion

The following are selected non-words examples specifically for **insertion** of alphabet that are passed through the proposed system to get candidate results:

Test word اصلاحت

Candidate word(s) اصلاحات [Other candidates are removed]

Action: ا is inserted between ح and ت

Deletion

The following are selected non-words examples specifically for **deletion** of alphabet that are passed through the proposed system to get candidate results:

Test word الجتھاؤ

Candidate word(s) الجھاؤ

Suggested word الجھاؤ

Substitution

The following are selected non-words examples specifically for **Substitution** of alphabet that are passed through the proposed system to get candidate results:

Test word قیسا

Candidate word(s) پیدا میرا ایسا

لیتا جیسا نیسب قیاس

Suggested word جیسا

Transposition

The following are selected non-words examples specifically for **Transposition** of two adjacent alphabets that are passed through the proposed system to get candidate results:

Test word بنلد

Candidate word(s) بٹلر بلند بند

Suggested word بلند

==================================

We have noticed that the transposition errors are poorly corrected using reverse edit distance as compared to edit distance algorithm. In above results, the words قیلل, پچیھے, تبیدل are not properly corrected by the algorithm.

6 Conclusion

Urdu language has rich literature, sponken in south asia, however having scarce resources in context of computer based applications. In this work, focus is on spelling error detection and correction feature in these electronic applications. Our this work is concentrated on gathering various spell checking and correction techniques that are suitable for correcting Urdu spelling errors . Reverse Edit Distance algorithm complexity is computed to be 86n + 41. The algorithm has been implememnted in other languages like English, and has to be implemented for Urdu.

References

Sara Stymne, Spell Checking Techniques for Replacement of Unknown Words and Data Cleaning for Haitian Creole SMS Translation, Association for Computational Linguistics, *Proceedings of the 6th Workshop on Statistical Machine Translation*, pages 470–477, Edinburgh, Scotland, UK, July 30–31, 2011.

Kemal Oflazer and Cemaleddin, Spelling correction in agglutinative languages. In *Proceedings of the fourth conference on Applied natural language processing (ANLC '94)*. Association for Computational Linguistics, Stroudsburg, PA, USA, 1994.

Fred J. Damerau. 1964. A technique for computer detection and correction of spelling errors. Commun. ACM 7, 3 (March 1964), 171-176. DOI=10.1145/363958.363994.

Tahira Naseem A Hybrid Approach for Urdu Spell Checking, MS Thesis 2004.

David Gries et al. Presenting an algorithm to find the minimum edit distance Department of Computer Science, Cornell University NSF Project 1988.

Eric Brill and Robert C. Moore, Microsoft Research, An Improved Error Model for Noisy Channel Spelling Correction YR + JNL.

M. D. Kernighan, K. W. Church, and W. A. Gale. A spelling correction program based on a noisy channel model. In Proceedings of the 13th International Conference on Computational Linguistics, volume 2, 1990.

O. Matan, C. J. C. Burges, Y. LeCun, and J. S. Denker. Multi-digit recognition using a space displacement neural network, Neural Information Processing Systems, volume 4, pages 488{495. Morgan Kaufmann Publishers, San Mateo,C.A., 1992.

V. J. Hodge and J. Austin. A comparison of standard spell checking algorithms and a novel binary neural approach. IEEE Transactions on Knowledge and Data Engineering, 2003.

Sarmad Hussain, Resources for Urdu Language Processing, Center for Research in Urdu Language Processing

Information Mining from Muslim Scriptures

Abdul Rauf Saeed
PUCIT, University of the Punjab
Lahore, Pakistan
bsef09m037@pucit.edu.pk

Syed Waqar Jaffry
PUCIT, University of the Punjab
Lahore, Pakistan
swjaffry@pucit.edu.pk

Abstract

There are billions of believers of various religions in the world and Islam is the second largest religion having 1.6 billion followers. The primary written sources of religious beliefs and practices of Muslims are the Quran and the Hadith (saying and practices of their prophet Muhammad Peace Be Upon Him). Written text of the Quran and the Hadith books is of manageable size and hence state of the art text mining techniques can easily be applied on it. In this paper first a comprehensive review of existing applications offering various type of the Quran and the Hadith information retrieval is presented then a framework based on text mining techniques is proposed. Finally an application is developed to demonstrate the Quran and the Hadith information retrieval framework. This application is evaluated with the help of an end user assessment questionnaire. It is recorded that end users have observed salient advantages of the designed application.

1 Introduction

There are several living religions in the world and the Islam is the second largest religion with respect to its followers (Ali, S. R., Liu, W. M., Humedian, M., 2004). Millions of Muslims (believers of Islam) receive their inspirations for the primary source of their religious beliefs and daily practices from the holy book "Quran" and sayings of their prophet Muhammad (PBUM) called "Hadith". Textual data stored in the Quran and the Hadith books is not huge and could be processed efficiently using the state of the art text analytic techniques. These machine based text processing techniques have the potential to summarize, analyze and effectively present different concepts present in these books. In this paper an initial effort based on research and implementation of a framework is presented which can help in processing and understanding this data. This paper also includes end users evaluation and author's conclusion and future work regarding this ongoing project. It is believed that this work would be useful for the researchers, and implementers who want to conduct similar research and development.

2 Related Work

The related work done on this field is very limited and can be extended further. Currently, most of the Quran and Hadith information retrieval systems are not well-formed as these systems search on basis of book name, volume number and the Hadith number and in case of the Quran it is the Surah (chapter) name or number and verse number. These kinds of systems are using primitive type of parameterized information retrieval. There are various systems like "The Islamic Search", "SearchTruth", "Allah.pk", "Islamic City", "IslamicSearch.org" and "IntoIslam" etc. The features of these systems and their working are briefly discussed as follows.

- The Islamic Search (TheIslamicSearch, 2013): It is an Islamic information retrieval system that takes a query from the user and it did not give results from Quran or Hadith but from the web by searching query with respect to some Islamic keywords (such as "Islamic", "Hadith", "Quran", "Islam" etc.). So, basically, it is not a information retrieval system based on the Quran and the Hadith but it is based on Google web search engine.
- SearchTruth (SearchTruth, 2013): It is a system that searches on the basis of exact keyword and the substring matching. For example, if we will search word "ski" instead of "sky", it will give Hadith or verse contains "asking".

- Allah.pk (Allah.pk, 2013): It is a search engine that searches the results on the basis of exact keyword matching. If the user enters wrong spelling or any word that is not present in the Quran or the Hadith, it will display no record found. Its plus point is that user can search in Arabic also and its results both in Arabic verse and its English translation.
- Islami City (IslamiCity, 2013): is a search engine that searches on the basis of keywords and give results. The searching only involves exact string matching in translation of the Quran. In results, the Arabic verse, its translation and phonetic verse is shown as well.
- Into Islam (intoIslam, 2013): is search engine similar to "The Islamic Search" in which user's query is searched through Google search API.

These are the well-known information retrieval systems based on the text of Quran and Hadith. It is observed that these all systems lack even primitive preprocessing and result ranking techniques used in information retrieval systems. Web Search Engines like Google are the examples of information retrieval systems. Hence the framework presented in this paper uses stemming and related algorithms to create inverted index and term frequency and inverted document frequency (TF-IDF) for result ranking. Furthermore proposed system uses synonyms for user query expansion to generated relevant results.

3 Methodology

This section provides a brief about the methodology followed in this research which includes data collection, preprocessing and the methods used for storage, searching and ranking of the results.

3.1 Data Collection

Three books of Hadith and the Quran are used. Hadith books include Sahih-Bukhari, Sahih-Muslim and Sunan-abi-Dawood. Texts for these books are taken from (Bihar Anjuman, 2013).

3.2 Data Pre-processing

In data pre-processing, first these books are converted from pdf files to text files in order to use these files in programming easily (Convertonlinefree.com, 2013). An online converter is used to convert the pdf files to text files. Furthermore, names of narrators are extracted from these Hadith books after tokenizing the words in file. Porter Stemmer algorithm (Porter, 1980) is used to stem the words.

After creating an index for Narrators the primary data set is again used to extract candidate keywords by applying RAKE keyword extraction algorithm. RAKE (Rapid Automatic Keyword Extraction) algorithm is used for extracting keyword from individual documents. In this algorithm, text is basically split on the basis of stop words and then a score is assigned to each phrase in the document. Stop words are the words that have higher frequency in text but they are just useless and cannot be used as a keyword for searching in the text such as (is, am, a, are, in etc.). After keyword extraction, the inverted index is created. Inverted index is a structure in which data is stored as key/value pair. In this structure, extracted keywords are placed as key and the list of indexes (locations in respective data file) is placed as value.

3.3 Method

There are three basic modules in this framework that are Hadith searching, Quran searching and searching from the both modules.

The first module is to search the Hadith. In this module, the user selects the book, narrator name and then enters query. As the user clicks 'search' button, the narrator name and query words are passed to a function where the query words are preprocessed. Preprocessing consists of conversion of text to upper case, removal of stop words, obtaining list of synonyms for each word and then stemming of each word. When the query is preprocessed the system gets the query word by word and gets the index(es) of each word and of its synonyms from the inverted index table. After getting the indexes, the system searches for the index values in Hadith books. After getting index value, it extracts whole Hadith and check the Narrator name. If it gets the combination of "NARRATED" and "NARRATOR NAME" in any line, it starts storing the Hadith in a variable and adds the variable in a list and again start searching for next index until the end of indexes. Now the list contains all the Hadith that is narrated by narrator selected by the user and related to user query. The list is then iterated for calculating the TF-IDF of all selected Hadith. The formula for calculating TF-IDF is mentioned below:

$$TF\text{-}IDF = TF(t, d) * IDF(t, D)$$

TF (t, d) = frequency of token *t* in document *d*

IDF (t, D) = log (|D| / {d in D, t in d})

Where,

t = token (word)
d = a specific document
D = all documents

In the above formula TF is equal to the ratio of frequency of each query word and its synonym in each Hadith to overall frequency of word in all Hadith. IDF is calculated by taking ratio of total Hadith to the count of Hadith in which the specific word found and then taking *log* of this ratio returns the IDF. Now, TF-IDF is calculated by taking product of TF and IDF for each word and Hadith. The list data is then sorted in descending order of their TF-IDF score and the final results are shown to the user.

In Quran searching, the user selects the Surah of Quran and then enters the query. The query is then pre-processed as mentioned above and the TF-IDF is calculated between query words and verses of the Quran. The verses are then sorted in descending order of TF-IDF score and finally the results are shown.

In searching from Quran and Hadith, both above mentioned methods are applied together. Detailed follow chart of the system is depicted in figure 1.

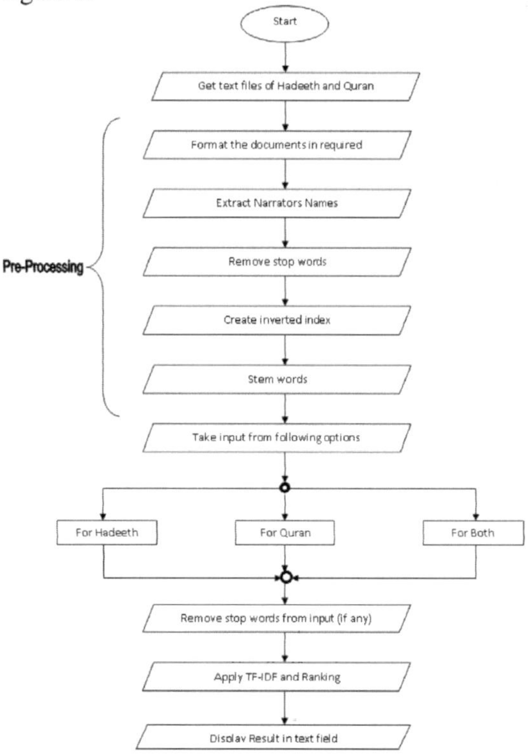

Figure 1. System Flow Diagram

4 Results

Results are measured on the basis of efficiency and usability. The following sections provide the details about results of both types.

4.1 Efficiency

For efficiency, time is noted for five cases, when number of query words range from one to five. The graph in figure 2 shows the time taken in seconds (y-axis) for the number of words in user query (x-axis). Here it can be observed that relationship between query size and the time taken by the system is linear.

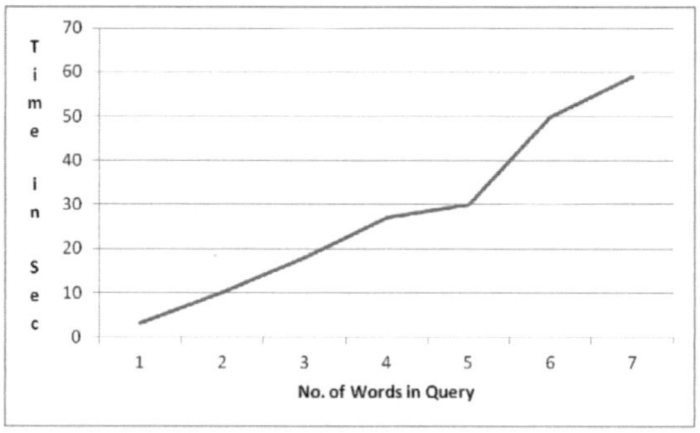

Figure 2. Performance

4.2 Usability

Usability results generated through a survey on Schneider Man's Principles based questionnaire (Shneiderman's, B. 2004). Questionnaire contains six questions with three options scaled to 0, 0.5 and 1. The following table shows results of questionnaire filled by ten participants, here column header should be read as, A: User ID, B: Layout Consistency, C: Easy to Understand, D: Organization of Actions, E: Error Prevention, F: Memorability, G: User Control, H: Informative Feedback, I: Use of Up to date Art.

A	B	C	D	E	F	G	H	I
1	1	1	1	1	0.5	1	0.5	1
2	1	1	1	1	1	0.5	0.5	0.5
3	1	0.5	1	1	0.5	0.5	1	0.5
4	1	0.5	1	1	1	0.5	0.5	1
5	1	1	0.5	0.5	0.5	0.5	0.5	1
6	0.5	0.5	1	1	0.5	0	0	0.5
7	1	1	1	1	0.5	0.5	1	0.5
8	1	1	1	1	1	1	1	1
9	0.5	0.5	0	0	0.5	1	0.5	0.5
10	1	1	0.5	0.5	1	0.5	0.5	1

Table 1. Usability Survey Results

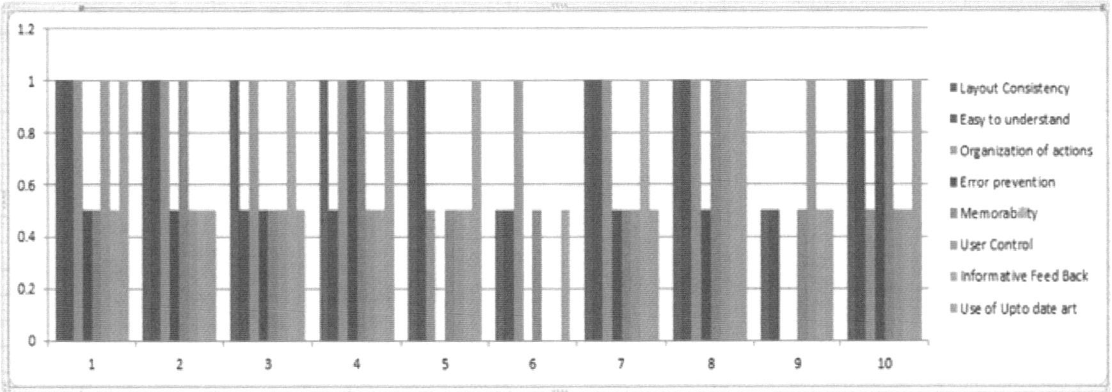

Figure 3. Usability Statistics

Results of this survey shows that users are more satisfied with first four indictors (B: Layout Consistency, C: Easy to Understand, D: Organization of Actions, E: Error Prevention) as compared to last four (F: Memorability, G: User Control, H: Informative Feedback, I: Use of Up to date Art). In future extensions specific consideration would be given to improve these factors. A usability graph generated from above table id shown in figure 3. This graph shows the variations of different questions by different participants.

5 Discussion

This work is a step to contribute in the field of text mining to process religious information particularly from Islamic Scriptures e.g. Quran and Hadith. In this paper searching of the Quran and Hadith with the options of synonyms matching and stemming the words has been introduced. For example, if a text contains 'happy' for five times and 'glad' for twenty times then user would be interested to view all these twenty five results, if s/he queries 'happy'. Also if search for the word 'pray' is generated then system will give results which contain the words like 'prays', 'praying' and 'prayed'. These two things make this work novel as current Quran and Hadith search engines do not offer such functionalities.

This research work can spawn several ideas and can provide a basis for further research on text mining in religious text. The extraction of information from Quran is a very vast task as it is believed that Quran and Hadith covers guidelines related to all aspects of human life including natural and related sciences beside the religious guidelines of morality and ethics. Hence this research of extracting information from Quran and Hadith has importance beyond religious boundaries.

6 Recommendations and Future Work

Some of the enhancements in current work include the better visualization of query results and the addition of more search options that can make user's experience more informative and rewarding. Such extensions might include, parametric, and chronological search support. Furthermore perspectives of different narrators and historians might be included and mined to provide different opinions of religious scholars on user's desired subject of search. Also current search can be extended from byword phrases to NLP query interface where the user can enter any query and system can detect the syntax as well as semantics of query in order to make the search results more relevant. In future this system can also be extended and multi-lingual support can be provided so that users can easily view and search results according in their native language. Another interesting future extension is to make a comparison among different Hadith and Verses to find out their mutual conflict or resemblances The Quran and the Hadith text can also be clustered among different hierarchies which can provide relations between concepts described in the text.

References

Alkhatib, M. 2010. *Classification of Al-Hadith Al-Sharif Using Data Mining Algorithm*, Proc. of European, Mediterranean & Middle Eastern Conference on Information Systems, Abu Dhabi.

Al-Kabi, M.and Al-Sinjilawi, S. 2007, *A comparative study of the efficiency of different measures to classify Arabic text*, University of Sharjah Journal of Pure and Applied Sciences, volume 4, No. 2.

Ali, S. R., Liu, W. M., Humedian, M. 2004. Islam 101: *Understanding the Religion and Therapy Im-*

plications. Professional Psychology: Research and Practice, Vol 35(6), 635-642.

Allah.pk. 2013. *The Multilingual Quran & Hadith Search Engine*, retrieved: 10-July-13.

Bihar Anjuman. 2013. *Bihar Anjuman – My RAHBAR*, retrieved: 17-June-13.

intoIslam.com, 2013. *intoIslam - Islamic Search Engine*, retrieved: 10-July-13.

IslamiCity.com, 2013. *Islam & The Global Muslim eCommunity*, retrieved: 10-July-13.

Jbara, K. 2010. *Knowledge Discovery in Al-Hadith Using Text Classification Algorithm*, Journal of American Science, 6(11).

Porter, M. 1980. *An Algorithm for Sufix Stripping*, Program, Vol. 14(3), pp. 130-137.

SearchTruth.com, 2013. Search Engine: Search in the Quran ال قران ال كري م and Hadith, retrieved: 10-July-13.

Shneiderman, B. 2004. Designing for fun: how can we design user interfaces to be more fun? interactions 11(5), 48-50.

TextMiningTheQuran.com. 2013. *Wiki textmining-thequran*, retrieved: 17-June-2013.

TheIslamicSearch.come, 2010. *ISLAMIC SEARCH powered by GOOGLE - Islamic Search Engine*, retrieved: 10-July-13.

Convertonlinefree.com 2013. *Free online PDF to TEXT converter*, retrieved: 17-June-2013.

Appendix A: Questionnaire for Usability Survey

1. Is Layout, color scheme, capitalization, font and menus consistency achieved in designing the interfaces?

   □ Yes
   □ No
   □ Up to Some Extent

2. Interface design and navigations are easy to understand for the diversified set of users?

   □ Yes
   □ No
   □ Up to Some Extent

3. For searching from anything, the actions performed are in sequence and organized (e.g. for searching, first click on searching option then select searching type then input fields and do search)?

   □ Yes
   □ No
   □ Up to Some Extent

4. Is there any mechanism for preventing any type of error (syntax or semantic error) like drop down list, autocomplete, suggestions etc.?

   □ Yes
   □ No
   □ Up to Some Extent

5. Is User feeling easy to do new things that what he/she is not told?

   □ Yes
   □ No
   □ Up to Some Extent

6. Is User feeling easy in reversal of step i.e. going back to previous states easily?

   □ Yes
   □ No
   □ Up to Some Extent

7. Is User feeling that he/she can easily control the system?

   □ Yes
   □ No
   □ Up to Some Extent

8. Is the display is simple i.e. user can memorize the steps easily?

   □ Yes
   □ No
   □ Up to Some Extent

9. Is the system giving response for every action either it is modest or complex depends on action?

   □ Yes
   □ No
   □ Up to Some Extent

10. Any up-to-date art/technique is used in this system?

    □ Yes
    □ No
    □ Up to Some Extent

Appendix B: System Screen Shots

Figure 4. Main Screen

Figure 5. The Hadith Search Interface

Figure 6. The Quran Search Interface

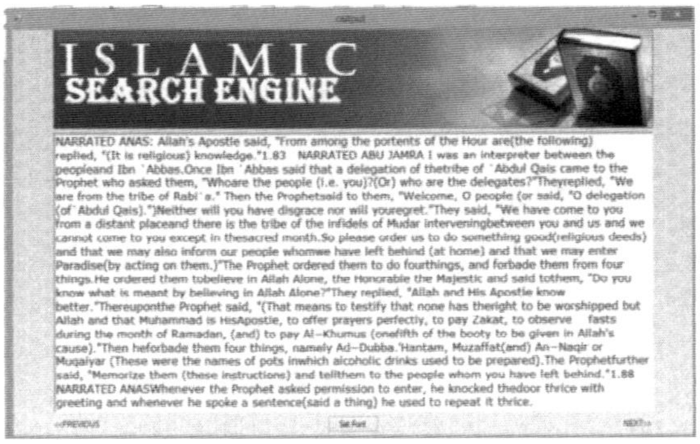

Figure 6. Search Results

English to Urdu
Hierarchical Phrase-based Statistical Machine Translation

Nadeem Khan [1] **Waqas Anwar**[1] **Usama Ijaz Bajwa** [1] **Nadir Durrani** [2]
[1]COMSATS Institute of Information Technology, Abbottabad Pakistan
[2]University of Stuttgart
[1] {nadeemk,waqas,usama}@ciit.net.pk, [2]durrani@ims.uni-stuttgart.de

Abstract

This paper addresses the Hierarchical Phrase-based (HPB) models which are used in development of different Statistical Machine Translation (SMT) Systems for many modern languages.
Any SMT System needs large parallel corpora for accurate performance. Therefore, availability of a large parallel corpus is a pre-requisite for designing a reliable, robust SMT system between any two languages. The HPB models have shown strong capability of generalization and reordering, which in turn gets improved results for the sparse resourced languages.
This paper considers English as Source and Urdu as target language for experiments. For this study, Hierarchical phrase-based Baseline SMT system is used for English to Urdu translation. At the end automatic evaluation of system is performed by using BLEU and NIST as evaluation metrics. Average BLEU evaluation score the developed system got is 13% which is a good competitive score for any sparse resourced language.

Keywords: HPB model, Statistical Machine Translation, Parallel corpus, Natural Language Processsing.

1 Introduction

Urdu is the national language of Pakistan, and also one of the spoken languages in India and is written in Perso-Arabic script. Urdu consists of many words which come from several languages, including Arabic, Persian and Turkish. English and Urdu, although both belong to the Indo-European language family, word order and morphology have very different characteristics for these two languages.

Both languages have different morphological and syntactic features. Urdu is highly inflectional language hence is rich in morphology. In Urdu the verbs are inflected according to gender, number, and person. English is a fixed word order language and follows the SVO (subject verb object) structure while Urdu is a free word order language and the most common sentence structure used by the native speakers is SOV (subject object verb). Also, instead of English prepositions, Urdu nouns and verbs are followed by postpositions. The above discussion emphasizes the differences between source language English and the target language Urdu.

Hierarchical phrase-based machine translation (Chiang, 2007; Watanabe et al., 2006) belongs to the current dominant and promising statistical machine translation approaches influenced by (Brown et al., 1993). Although the model captures, global reordering SCFG (Synchronous context-free grammar), the reordering does not explicitly introduces the model to restrict word order. On the contrary, the lexicalized reordering models (Tillman, 2004; Nagata et al., 2006) are often used for the translation on the Phrase-based models. These lexicalized reordering models cannot be applied directly to hierarchical phrase-based translation, because the representation of the hierarchical phrase translation uses the nonterminal symbols.

Hierarchical phrase-based statistical machine translation (Chiang, 2007) has shown the competition between phrase-based and syntax-based models for different language pairs. An important issue with hierarchical set-based translation, the size of the model on which training is carried out, which is usually several times larger than the trained phrase-based counterpart from the same dataset. This leads to over generation search errors and a slow decoder (de Gispert et al., 2010). In this work, the main focus is on hierarchical models usage in SMT, focused on the expression of (Chiang,.2007), which is officially based on the syntax, and always consult the term SCFG.

HPB SMT (Chiang, 2005) is a tree-based model that automatically extracts a synchronous CFG from the training corpus. HPB SMT extracted hierarchical rules, the basic units of translation in the HPB model phrases extracted according to the PB model (Koehn et al., 2003). So, hierarchical rules have the strengths of the statistically extracted continuous sets plus the ability to translate interrupted sentences too and learn sentence reordering without a separate reordering model. The HPB SMT model has two kinds of rules: hierarchical rules and glue grammar rules. Hierarchical set-based translation (Chiang, 2005; Chiang,2007) expand highly lexicalized-Based models of sentence translation systems lexicalized rearrangement model and disjoint sets. A major drawback with this approach compared to set-based systems is that the total number of rules that are learned are several orders of magnitude larger than standard tables, which leads to over-generation rate and help search error and too much longer decoding time. Chiangs hierarchical phrase-based (HPB) translation model uses SCFG for translation free derivation (Chiang, 2005; Chiang, 2007) and has been widely accepted in SMT.

2 Previous Work

Various work with different approaches have been proposed for many Subcontinent Languages in the field of machine translation when translating from English into anyone of these languages or when discussing the divergence in translation of anyone of these languages specially for Hindi.

(Chiang et.al.2005) proposed Hierarchical Phrase-Based Model for SMT for different European languages, that can be made applicable for sparse resourced languages by having some tuning on the model.

(Jawaid et.al,.2011) investigated phrase-based statistical machine translation between English and Urdu, two Indo-European languages that differ significantly in their word-order preferences. They showed reordering of words and phrases is a necessary part of the translation process. While local reordering is modeled nicely by phrase-based systems. Again long-distance reordering is known to be a hard problem. They performed experiments using the Moses SMT system. They also presented an Urdu aware approach based on reordering phrases in syntactic parse tree of the source English sentence.

(Singh et.al. 2004) proposed an approach for English to Bangla MT that uses syntactic transfer of English sentences to Bangla with optimal time complexity. In generation stage they used a dictionary to identify subject, object and also other information like person, number and generate target sentences.

(Singh,.2012) presented a Phrase based model approach to English-Hindi translation. In this work they discussed the simple implementation of default phrase-based model for SMT for English to Hindi and also give an overview of different Machine translation application that are in use nowadays

(Sharma et.al.2011) presented a baseline Phrase-based system for English to Hindi Translation with a pretty small amount of data. They used human evaluation metrics as their evaluation measures. These evaluations cost higher than the already available automatic evaluation metrics.

(Islam et al.2010) proposed a phrase-based Statistical Machine Translation (SMT) system that translates English sentences to Bengali. They added a transliteration module to handle OOV (Out of Vocabulary) words. A preposition handling module is also incorporated to deal with systematic grammatical differences between English and Bangla. To measure the performance of their system, they used BLEU, NIST and TER scores as their evaluation metrics. The dataset collected from KDE and EMILLE corpus.

By having a look at the work above, It is clear that there is not a single proposed work when talking about one of the important language of South Asia namely Urdu.

3 Evaluation

This section discusses the training, tuning and testing of different model components. The evaluation was carried on Ubuntu 11.10 running on Intel Core i3 machine with 4GB of RAM and 500GB of Hard disk space.

3.1 Dataset

We used the EMILLE (Enabling Minority Language Engineering) corpus. EMILLE was a 3 year EPSRC project at Lancaster University and Sheffield University. Its final output was an elec-

tronic corpus of 97 million words of South Asian languages and is becoming a standard data repository for the languages of this region.
The parallel corpus consists of 200,000 words of text in English and its accompanying translations in Hindi, Bengali, Punjabi, Gujarati and Urdu. Its bilingual resources consists of roughly above 12,500 sentences for all the available languages.
We were able to do sentence alignment and extract over 8,000 sentence for our required language pair i.e. English and Urdu using the sentence alignment algorithm given by (Moore.,2002).In any SMT development project making of parallel corpus is the most complicated task.
EMILLE corpus is the most rough available corpus ever seen for languages of this region. Cleaning of this corpus for making it completely compatible and sentence aligned, is the very first step and also the toughest one that is used in the development of any SMT system. Further details about parallel data are given in Table 1.

Total Sentences	Training	Tuning	Testing
8245	6596	825	824

Table 1: Complete Statistics of Parallel Corpus

The monolingual resources used in the development of language model for this study work consists of overall 40,000 above segments in which there are target parallel corpus of Urdu with corpus of Quran and Bible that is available for free on web.

3.2 Experimental Setup

The k-fold cross validation method was used for sampling of the corpus. Here k=5 was selected by taking 4/5 of the total corpus as training and 1/5 as tuning and test set for experiment on all folds. Each fold comprises roughly above 800 tuning and same number of sentences for testing along with above 6500 sentences for training. After sampling of data, tokenization of training set, tuning set and test set is done for all folds dataset followed by lowercasing of datasets. All this is done by the scripts being supplied with the Moses decoder (Koehn et al., 2007). This lowercased training data is used for word alignment. As the overall training data is very sparse, so there is no need to use clean-out script for cleaning long sentences from the training data before training the system.
We ran Moses (Koehn et al., 2007) using Koehn's training scripts. In our work additional switches like hierarchical and glue-grammar are also used in training command as the experiments are being done with the HPB model. For the other parameters, the default values were used i.e. 3-gram language model and maximum phrase-length= 6. The word alignments for the system are extracted by using GIZA++ (Och and Ney, 2003) that is linked with the training script of Moses.
Language Model is built on the available monolingual Urdu corpus. This language model is implemented as an n-gram model using the SRILM Toolkit. For all the experiments, the same language model is used for all folds as translation is being performed from English into Urdu. System tuning for the extraction of optimized feature weights that would be used in testing of the developed system is done by using MERT (Och, 2003).
When it comes to testing, the testing phase was completed by using the Moses decoder. Note that the command used here is moses-chart instead of moses. This is because the work is being carried out with hierarchical-phrase based model. This testing is done in the same way for all fold test sets.

3.3 Results

All the evaluation scores and some sample translations from the developed SMT system are given in this section:
As working on a sparse resourced language, we have achieved much better BLEU scores with a mean of 0.132 and a Standard deviation of 0.09 for the entire given test sets. Overall results of BLEU and NIST evaluation score for all folds are given below in Table: 2 and 3 respectively.
A comparison of the developed Hierarchical Phrase-based translation system with the traditional Phrase-based system was also carried out. It can be noted from Table 2 and 3 the traditional Phrase-based model system got better BLEU and NIST scores as compared to the Hierarchical Phrase-based model approach for this language pair. This is because of the morphological richness and the divergence of Urdu with English. Another important factor that is causing this small difference between the results of two models is the sparseness of corpus for this language pair as we got such a small size of corpus in our experiments.
From Table 2, It can be noted the sudden change occurred in BLEU score for fold-5 of both the tra-

ditional Phrase-based system as well as our Hierarchical Phrase-based system, this change is due to the relevance in domains of test and training dataset.

Folds	f1	f2	f3	f4	f5
Phrase-based	0.11	0.08	0.12	0.13	0.40
Hierarchical	0.09	0.06	0.10	0.10	0.29

Table 2: Comparison of BLEU evaluation score with traditional Phrase-based model

Folds	f1	f2	f3	f4	f5
Phrase-based	3.52	3.25	3.92	4.27	7.36
Hierarchical	3.42	3.26	3.80	4.16	6.36

Table 3: Comparison of NIST evaluation score with traditional Phrase-based model

From the BLEU and NIST evaluation score results above, It can be noted clearly how much sparseness and difference in domain of datasets within all 5 folds.In BLEU score, fold-5 got the highest percentage of result i.e. 29%, and in other fold there is not a single result greater than 10% for our Hierarchical Phrase-based system, this is because of the difference in domains of training and testing corpus. In fold-5 the test data become pretty much closer to the domains of dataset on which system is actually trained.
Figure 1 shows how the decoder perform translations of the test dataset using the chart decoder for Hierarchical Phrase-based model.

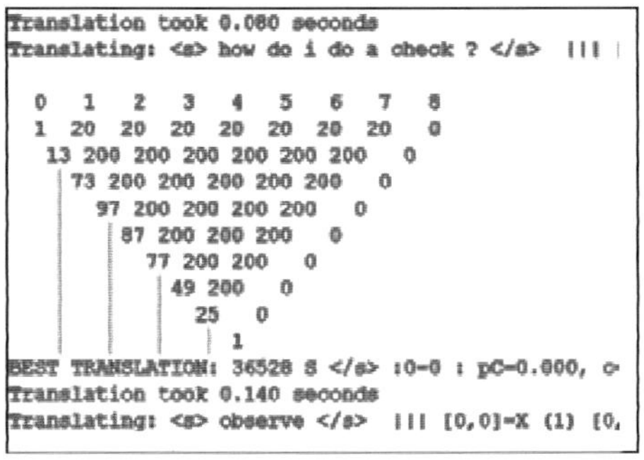

Figure 1: Working of Hierarchical Phrase-based decoder.

Some example of translation generated by our developed English-Urdu translation system are given in Table 4. There is much difference in ordering of words in some sentences like in third sentence from the Table 4, the decoder did not

Input English Sentence	Output Urdu Sentence
Parent Partnership Service	والدین شراکت سروس
you are aged 60 or over	آپ کی عمر 60 سال یا اس سے زیادہ
Not working,or working on average less than 16 hours a week?	کام نہیں، یا ہفتے میں اوسطا 16 گھنٹے ؟
How to claim see page 30.	کلیم کیسے کیا جائے دیکھیے صفحہ30.
Working with the court	عدالت کے ساتھ کام

Table 4: Translations generated by our system.

changed the order of words while translating in Urdu, it just translated the words one by one from English side and give us completely out of order output on Urdu side.

4 Conclusion

In this work we explored one of the important but relatively less addressed research problems. As Urdu has got rich morphology and its inflectional behavior is also very variable, therefore, an extensively sparse corpus for experiments was used. Also because of the sparseness of the corpus, the evaluation results are not that much impressive as compared to those for some of the European languages.
In this work Hierarchical Phrase-based model for training was employed. We carried out a set of experiments by choosing the training, tuning and test sets from parallel corpus using the k-fold cross validation method to cater for the fact that we had only a small amount of parallel data. We found that our targeted language Urdu has got pretty much divergence when translating from English and that is the reason for that much difference in obtained MT evaluation scores on our given test-sets.

References

Andreas Stolcke 2002. *SRILM - an extensible language modeling toolkit.*. In International Conference Spoken Language Processing, Denver, Colorado.

Adri a de Gispert et.al 2010. *Hierarchical phrase-based translation with weighted finite-state transducers and shallow-n grammars.*. In Proceedings of Association of Computational Linguistics.

Brown. P et.al 1993. *The mathematics of statistical*

machine translation: Parameter estimation.. In Proceedings of Association of Computational Linguistics.

Bushra Jawaid et.al 2011. *Word-Order Issues in English-to-Urdu Statistical Machine Translation.*. The Prague Bulletin of Mathematical Linguistics.

Chiang, D 2005. *A hierarchical phrase-based model for statistical machine translation.*. In Proceedings of Association of Computational Linguistics.

Chiang, D 2007. *Hierarchical phrase-based model for statistical machine translation.*. In Proceedings of Association of Computational Linguistics.

Dharvendra Singh et al 2012. *Modelling Phrase-Based Statistical Machine Translation for English-Hindi Language.*. IJRREST: International Journal of Research Review in Engineering Science and Technology

Franz J. Och 2003. *Minimum Error Rate Training in Statistical Machine Translation.* In 41st Annual Meeting of the Association for Computational Linguistics (ACL 2003), Sapporo, Japan.

Franz J. Och and Hermann Ney 2003. *A systematic comparison of various statistical alignment models.*. In Proceedings of Association of Computational Linguistics.

Maxim Roy. 2009. *A Semi-supervised Approach to Bengali-English Phrase-Based Statistical Machine Translation,* . Proceedings of the 22nd Canadian Conference on Artificial Intelligence

Nagata et al 2006. *A clustered global phrase reordering model for statistical machine translation.*. In Proceedings of Association of Computational Linguistics.

Nakul Sharma, Parteek Bhatia and Varinderpal Singh 2011. *English to Hindi Statistical Machine Translation.*. International Journal in Computer Networks and Security (IJCNS).

Philip Koehn, Franz J. Och and D.Marcu . 2003. *Statistical Phrase-Based Translation* . In HLT-NAACL 2003: conference combining Human Language Technology conference series and the North American Chapter of the Association for Computational Linguistics conference series, Edmonton, AB, 2003.

Philip Koehn et.al 2005. *Edinburgh system description for 2005 IWSLT speech translation evaluation.*. In Proceedings. the 2nd IWSLT.

Philip Koehn et.al 2007. . *Moses: Open Source Toolkit for Statistical Machine Translation.*. Annual Meeting of the Association for Computational Linguistics (ACL).

Robert C. Moore 2002. *Fast and accurate sentence alignment of bilingual corpora,* . In Conference of the Association for Machine Translation in the Americas (AMTA).

Sajib Dasgupta, Abu Wasif and Sharmin Azam 2004. *An Optimal Way towards Machine Translation from English to Bengali.* Proceedings of the 7th International Conference on Computer and Information Technology (ICCIT).

Tillman. C 2004. *A unigram orientation model for statistical machine translation.*. In Proc. HLT-NAACL.

Watanabe, T. H. Tsukada, and H. Isozaki 2006. *Left-to-right target generation for hierarchical phrase-based translation.*. In Proceedings of Association of Computational Linguistics.

Zahurul Islam, Jrg Tiedemann and Andreas Eisele 2010. *English to Bangla Phrase Based Machine Translation.*. In the Proceedings of the 14th Annual Conference of The European Association for Machine Translation.

Cliticization and Endoclitics Generation of Pashto Language

Azizud Din
aziz621@gmail.com
Department of Computer and Information Sciences, Al Jouf University, KSA
Faculty of Computer Science and Information Technology, University Malaysia Sarawak, Malaysia

Abstract---**Pashto is one of the national languages of "Afghanistan", and the home language of Pushtuns living in the "Khyber Pakhtoonkhwa Province" of "Pakistan" and many Pushtuns living in Baluchistan. Pashto language allows pronominal clitics to be inserted into morphological words. The clitics with this property are called endoclitics. This paper describes an account of Pashto Endoclitics generation which is an early stage of generation, Cliticization rules and the unique challenge posed by these clitics to the traditional syntactic theory. Pashto endoclitics are interesting, because they cannot be completely accounted for by syntax or prosody alone, but transcend different levels of grammar framework. In a natural generation task, the problem of clitic generation has to deal with syntax, prosody, and discourse constraints.**

Index Terms---**Clitics, Cliticization, Endoclitic, Prosody , Syntax.**

I. Introduction

Pashto is spoken by about 13 million people in the south, east and a few northern provinces of Afghanistan and over 28 million in the province of Khyber Pakhtoonkhwa, Federally Administered Tribal Areas, and Baluchistan. Smaller, modern "transplant" communities are also found in Sindh (Karachi, Hyderabad). In the linguistics literature clitics are described as morphemes that are neither independent words nor morphological affixes. Syntactically and phonologically clitics follow the host word to which they are attached. Clitics are grouped into four types: proclitics, enclitics, meesoclitics, and endoclitics. Proclitics are prefixed to host word; enclitics are suffixed to host word; and mesoclitics appear between the stem of the host word and other affixes. Endoclitics are inserted inside the host root stem by splitting the root stem into semantically deficient parts. Pashto allows all of these types of clitics to occur in sentences. Pashto has been written in a variant of the Persian script (which in turn is a variant of Arabic script) since the late sixteenth century [1].

Pashto clitics normally occurs in the second position (2P) of a clause or sentence [2], however they may occur in various other positions in sentences as well, but never occurs at the beginning of a sentence as the following examples show.

دي   ورور   دي   وقاص
de   *wroor*   *<u>dee</u>*   *waqas*
aux   brother   CLT(yours)Waqas
Waqas is your brother.

لو ستو   دي   كتاب
lwasto   *<u>dee</u>*   *kitaab*
were reading   CLT   book
(You) were reading a book.

The following table gives a complete list of clitics used in Pashto language [3]. However, endoclitics generation in Pashto language occurs only with pronominal clitics *<u>mee</u>*, *<u>dee</u>* and *<u>yee</u>*, *am*.

Table I
Pashto clitics

Pashto Clitics	Gloss	Type
مي	**mee**	**Pronominal**
دي	**dee**	**Pronominal**
ي	**yee**	***Pronominal***
ام	**am**	**Pronominal**
مو	**mo**	**Pronominal**
به	ba	Modal
دي	de	Modal
خو	kho	Adverbial
نو	no	Adverbial
را	Ra	Oblique Pronominal
در	der	Oblique Pronominal
ور	*wer*	Oblique Pronominal

Pashto clitics display properties commonly attributed to *post-lexical* clitics as they are *prosodically* dependent on an adjacent prosodic element and co-occur with hosts from a limited set of syntactic categories. Tagey [4] derives the generalization that 2P Clitics appear after the *"First stress bearing"* phrasal constituent in the Pashto clause. The phrasal host must be stress-bearing and must contain at least one primary *accent*. 2P Clitics normally are not hosted by unaccented constituents. In general, it has been demonstrated in work done so far by other authors, that clitic placement in a phrase or a sentence is driven by syntactic, morphological and prosodic rules. The following example shows clitic occurring after a phrasal constituent. The unstressed material infront of the verb makes the clitic appear at the very right *edge of the phrase*.

[پیغله   خائسته   او   دنګه   کالو   شلو   د   اغه]
$_{NP}$ [*Peeghla khaaysta aw danga kaloo shaloo da aagha*]
[Girl pretty and tall years twenty postp that]$_{NP}$

ولیده بیا نن دي
Wa'lida Bya nen dee
Saw again today CLT-you

You saw that twenty years old tall and pretty girl again today.

The rest of the paper is organized as follows. In section II, we describe the related works about Pashto endoclitics generation with examples. Section III reviews Syntactic and Phonological Features of Clitics. In section IV, we presented clitics placement rules. Conclusions are presented in section V.

II. Pashto Endoclitics

Pashto allows clitics to be inserted into morphological words. The clitics with this property are called endoclitics. By definition endoclitics are inserted inside a word (verb in Pashto is split by endoclitic) by splitting the word into separate nonadjacent and semantically vacuous pieces. Endoclitics may not be regarded as morphological inflections as their semantics are unrelated to the host word in most of the cases. Morphologically endoclitics violate principle of *Lexical Integrity* (which states that syntactic operations may not interfere with morphology of words) [5]. The following example from [4] shows the occurrence of an endoclitic in a Pashto sentence with imperfective verb form.

اخستل ما
Akhist-el maa
buy$_{3sg}$ 1sg
I was buying them.(Tagey 1977:89)

Pashto is strictly a verb final language (word order in Pashto is SOV). The verb [akhist-el] appears non-finally and clitic [*mee*] occurs after it, because the clitic needs a host element if the strong pronoun ***maa*** is deleted. Sentences can thereby consist of simply a verb and a clitic.

مي اخستل
mee akhist-el
1SG buy3$_{sg}$
I was buying them.

Tagey observes that *a-initial* verbs can be split apart by clitics. Specifically, in the presence of a clitic the initial [a] of these verbs can split off from the rest of the verb root rendering the above sentence as show below. It is important to note that the part of verb appearing before the verb cannot be classified as either affix or an independent word.

خستل مي ا
Khist-el mee a
buy$_{3sg}$ CLT(I) ??
I was buying them.

Similarly, in the perfective form of the verb, the verb [akhistal] is prefixed with [wa] perfective marker resulting the following sentential form.

اخستل وا ما
Akhist-el wa maa
buy$_{3sg}$ PERF 1SG
I bought them.

In the above sentence, deleting the strong pronoun [maa] introduces the clitic [mee]. This is shown by the sentence below.

خستل مي ا وا
Khist-el mee a wa
buy$_{3sg}$ CLT ?? PERF
I bought them.

For explanatory purpose another example in which a clitic introduces as endoclitic is demonstrated by the following sentences.

خستل نه ا وا مي هغه
Khist-el na a wa mee agha
buy$_{3sg}$ not ?? PERF CLT(1sg) 3SG
I did not buy it.

ه واه و ي هغه
ah waha wa yee agha
AUX$_{3SG}$ beat PERF CLT(3sg) 3SG
He beats him.

Clitics always maintain second position. For example, if the strong pronoun [agha] is deleted from the second sentence above, the endoclitic would still be in second position after the perfective marker [wa], resulting in a sentence in which perfective marker [wa] (suffix) is no longer attached to the verb.

ه واه ي و
a *Waha yee wa*
Aux$_{3SG}$ best CLT(3sg) PERF
He beats him. (the pronoun agha deleted)

If the perfective marker [wa] is removed, the endoclitic is again placed in the second position, and moves to the last position in the sentence.

ي ه واه
yee a waha
CLT Aux$_{3SG}$ beat
He was beating him.

There is another example which illustrates the insertion of clitic between perfective marker and verb.

ولوله ي ته
walwala *<u>yee</u>* *ta*
read it(CLT) you
You read it.

When the strong pronoun [ta] is deleted, a new sentence is generated with endoclitic as shown below.

لوله ي و
lwaala *<u>yee</u>* *wa*
read it(CLT) PERF
You read it.

Pashto verb has been identified to play important role in clitic placement. Kopris describes following five different classes of verb that have different behaviors in the presence of endoclitics [5].

1. Imperfective and Perfective verb
2. *a*-initial verb
3. Simple verb
4. Derivative verb
5. Doubly irregular verb

In Bogel's analysis, endoclitics are subject to prosodic as well as syntactic constraints [6]. Prosodically, a clitic is placed after the first item bearing lexical stress in a sentence. Pashto is classified as an argument-dropping language, which is made possible by the syntactic agreement system on verbs and nouns. The endoclitics appear after aspect-caused stressed constituents. With regard to stress, Pashto verbs fall roughly into three classes, depending on their word-internal structure [6]. Bogel defines three classes of verbs with respect to clitics and endoclitics.

Class 1 Verbs: Monomorphemic imperfective verbs bear stress on the last syllable; the clitic is placed after the verb. *The perfective monomorphemic verbs* take on a perfective prefix [wa] that bears the main stress and the clitic occurs after the prefix. . The following shows an example.

مي تبنوله
<u>me</u> *texnawala*
CLT tickle
I was tickling (her). (Tagey 1977: 86)

In the perfective aspect the [wa] marker attaches to the verb as a prefix and clitic occurs after it. In this case [wa] prefix is stressed.

تبنوله مي و
texnawala *<u>me</u>* *wa*
tickle CLT PERF
I tickled (her). (Tagey 1977:92)

Class 2 Verbs: **(compound prefix + root):** These verbs form the perfective by means of a stress on the first syllable of the verb. A class-2 verb is bi-morphemic and is formed by a derivational prefix and a root. Syntactically these verbs are viewed as one unit.

Class 3 Verbs: **(compound lexical item + auxiliary verb)**: They are similar to class-2 verbs, but are complex predicates (light verb + adjective/adverb/noun). These verbs are also split by clitics as shown by the next two example sentences.

مي پوري وسته
<u>mee</u> *pore wasta*
1SG carry across(3sg,FEM,PAST)
I carried her across.

وسته مي پوري
Wasta *<u>mee</u>* *pore*
PERF 1SG Carry across
I carried her across.

It has been suggested by Tagey [4], that there is a separate group of *a-initial* verbs, which has nine verbs that start with vowel [a]. These verbs show a very distinct behavior with regard to optional stress in the imperfective aspect. These verbs are: [akhistal] 'to buy', [aleyal] 'to singe', [acawal] 'to throw', [agustal] 'to put on', [alwtal] 'to fly', [astawal] 'to send', [arawal] 'to turn over', [azmeyal] 'to test', and [awral] 'to hear'.

Some researchers have concluded that [a] was originally a prefix clitic [7], though [a] is no longer a recognizable prefix in Pashto. The class-2 and class-3 verbs can be thought of allowing clitic to be inserted post-lexically (at phonological level) into verb, without violating the principle of Lexical Integrity.

In the perfective tense, *a-initial* verbs take the perfective prefix [we] like all other class-1 verbs. Perfective *a-initial* verbs display vowel coalescence, a process that is assumed to take place in the lexicon. The *a-initial* verbs in class-1 undergo vowel coalescence when they are preceded by a particle ending in a vowel i.e. [we] [na] and [ma].The Pashto rule of vowel coalescence (VC) and its interaction with clitic placement was studied by Tegey [4]. The following example illustrates the vowel coalescence.

واخله ي ته
waxla *<u>yee</u>* *ta* **ta yee w**<u>aa</u>**xla*
buy_{PERF} it you
You buy it.

مه اخله ي ته
maxla *<u>yee</u>* *ta* **ta yee m**<u>aa</u>**xla*

not-buy it you
Don't buy it.

نه اخلي ي ته
naxla *yee* *ta*
no-buy it you **ta yee n**aa**xla*
Don't buy it.

The interaction of clitic and vowel coalescence is shown by the sentence below, as the clitic is inserted between vowel coalesced parts [wa] and [*staw-el*].

ستول وا مي نن
staw-el *wa* *mee* *none*
sent PERF CLT today
I sent them today.

ستول مي وا
staw -el *mee* *wa*
sent CLT PERF
I sent them.

Tegey supposed that a syntactic rule for clitic placement applied after phonological rule (vowel coalescence). According to Kassie the phonological motivation of VC is the elimination of haitus (phonological gapping) [8]. She suggests the following process for VC.

$[\text{ə}]_{particle} + [\text{a, ɑ}]_{verb} \rightarrow [\text{ɑ}]$

Kassie concludes that VC is a type of lexically restricted phonological process and only *a- for a-initial verbs* undergo VC [8]. Therefore *a-* is considered as a morphological prefix, thereby claiming that no verb stem begins with a vowel. The *a-initial* verbs are described as midway between class-1 and class-2, as they take the perfective particle, but contain a stressable prefix. Clitics never move in the syntax, but may only move in the phonology to find a host to their left by the process of *prosodic inversion*. Bogel concludes that clitics are inserted into the *morphological word* post lexically, and are subjected to prosodic constraints and stress [6]. Moreover she assumes that prosody inserts clitics post lexically after an accent-bearing element, thereby asserting that attachment to a host is *a strong prosodic constraint*.

III. Syntactic and Phonological Features of Clitics

The first detailed study of Pashto clitics was carried out by Tagey [4] in his Phd dissertation. Tagey proposed that the clitic placement was syntactic, without elaborating on the exact syntactic mechanisms that determine clitic placement. Kassiere affirmed that the Pashto clitics can be dealt with only syntax and morphology. In Tagey's analysis "clitics are placed after the first major surface constituent that bears at least one main stress". Apparently the suggestion posits that phonology interacts with syntax inorder to place clitics in correct position in sentences. In a later publication Muhammad and Babrakzai proposed that clitic placement can be treated as syntactic agreement [2]. According to Dost clitics placement within sentences and clauses is governed by constraints on syntax, prosody, lexical and sublexical levels, thereby blurring the distinction and interaction between these different levels [9].

In the analysis of Roberts, clitics are divided into two groups: one appearing in the *second position* of the clause, and another that appearing *nearer to the verb* [10]. In Robert's analysis Pashto 2P clitics identify oblique-case NPs (in ergative, accusative and genitive cases) and license null oblique-case arguments. Clitics do not intervene among conjuncts, and among the parts of any clause-initial constituent.

خو و اخستل مي [كاپی او كتاب]
Kho wakhist-el mee ConjP[copy aw kitaab]
Adv.CLT bought CLT-I notebook and book
I bought a notebook and a book but .....'

But the native speakers cannot speak it as below:

واخستل كاپی او مي كتاب
wakhist-el *copy* *aw* *mee* *kitab*
Bought notebook and CLT-1sg book
Or
واخستل كاپی مي او كتاب
wakhist-el *copy* *mee* *aw* *kitaab*
bought notebook CLT-1sg and book

The ordering of pronominal clitics within a cluster (a series of adjacent clitics) is determined by person feature *syntactically* instead of a morphological template. Clitics bear person and number features which are not unique. Possessive clitics are dislocated from overt nominal with which they are semantically associated. There is a strong relationship between strong pronouns and pronominal clitics as stated by Roberts [10]. Strong pronouns occur at the same positions as the full NPs, but discourse neutral (topic) pronouns tend to appear in the form of second position Clitics. Pashto clitics have been studied from pure phonological aspect as well [10]. Roberts attempted to incorporate Pashto clitics into Chomsky's Minimalist Program. He states that 2P pronominal clitics are agreement morphemes based on the observation (also made in [2]) that pronominal 2P Clitics are in complementary distribution with verbal agreement morphology. This leads to the prediction that only ergative and accusative arguments may be criticized, whereas nominative or absolutive arguments cannot be criticized. Each clitic heads an agreement projection, whose specifier licenses a null pronominal argument. As an example the constituent tree for the sentence [waqas me wanalide] *'I didn't not see Waqas (a person).'* is shown below from [9].

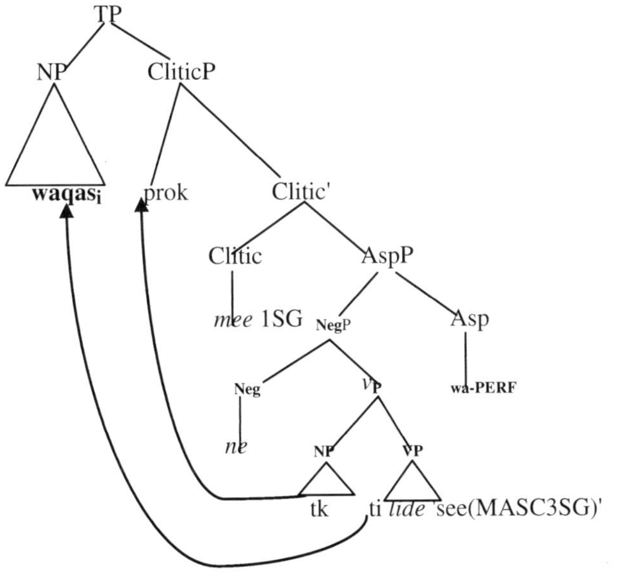

The NP leaves a trace and overtly moves to the subject position in the sentence thereby positioning itself with respect to clitic.

Dost [9] objects to the proposal brought forward by Roberts and identifies three problems with the syntax only analysis.

1. 2P clitics should be *double overt pronominal arguments* based on the agreement hypothesis ("clitics as agreement hypothesis"), but that do not.
2. The second problem is with endoclitics (that clitic in-fixation). Tagey in his analysis, identifies three classes of main verbs in Pashto, that sometimes require 2P Clitics to appear after the first *accented syllable* of the verb, rather than after the verb itself.When stress occurs on the first syllable of the verb (in perfective aspect), 2P Clitics obligatorily occur after the stressed syllable. According to Dost, Robert's analysis does not consider clitics to be another natural word class, but rather considers them agreement morphemes and wrongly predicts the behavior of endoclitics.
3. The third problem identified by Dost is that 2P Clitics are prosodically required to have hosts. This property is lost by the syntactic treatment and EPP (Extended Projection Principle: the requirement that clauses have subjects), which is a syntactic requirement and not a prosodic one.

According to Dost the hypothesis, that 2p clitics are agreement morphemes is wrong. The suggestion made by earlier studies that clitics should co-occur with full nominal arguments, is not supported by the actual linguistic data [6]. As an alternate Dost describes a *Domain Based Approach* to clitic placement in Head-Driven Phrase Structure Grammar (HPSG).

IV. CLITIC PLACEMENT

Pashto 2P clitics are unaccented, monosyllabic words that need single stressed phonological structure to their immediate left. According to existing clitic theories, Pashto clitics occur after first syntactic/prosodic structure in a sentence, which may be a word, phrase or prosodic unit. The first structure has to bear primary stress. Therefore, when placing clitics, syntax as well as prosodic constraints on phrases, words and units smaller than words have to be considered. Below Fig.1shows the sentence with strong pronoun on the top down parsing tree on the left side and with clitic on the right.

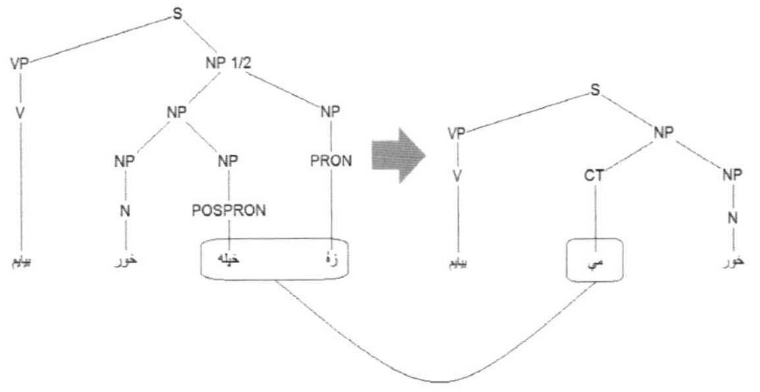

Figure 1. Cliticization

Clitics occur with wide range of syntactic hosts, and show low degree of selection with respect to hosts.

Table II specifies the rules for replacing strong pronouns with 2P (second position) clitics based on syntactic constraints only. This process is called cliticization. The abbreviations used in Table II are defined in Table III.

Table II
Rules for 2P Clitics

Rule	***Strong Pronoun***	***Syntactic Constraint***	***Replacement Clitic***
1	زه خپله	verb(sng, p1, present)	مې
2	زه خپل	dob(mas), verb(sng, p1, present)	مې
3	ما	verb(past)	مې
4	زما	verb(sng, p3, past)	مې
5	تاسو خپل	verb(past), mod(qst)	ام
6	ته خپل	dob(mas), verb(sng, p2, present)	دې
7	ته خپله	dob(fem), verb(sng, p2, present)	دې
8	تا	verb(past)	دې
9	ستا	verb(past)	دې
10	دَ هغه	verb(sng, p1, present)	ې
11	دَ هغوئ	verb(sng, p1, present)	ې
12	دَ هغي	verb(sng, p1, present)	ې

The rules specified in Table II use only syntactic knowledge of clitic placement to introduce a clitic at second position (2P) into a sentence by replacing an already existing strong pronoun within the sentence. These rules do not include Pashto endoclitics. Pure syntactic rules such as given in Table II cannot be formulated for the generation of endoclitics in a sentence, because of afore mentioned problems. To meet up with the challenge of endoclitic generation it is necessary to allow interaction between most notable linguistic levels; syntax and prosody during the generation of Pashto language text from any knowledge represented in computational form.

TABLE III
Abbreviations used in Table II

Abbreviations	*Definition*
Dob	Direct object in the current clause
Fem	Feminine
Mas	Masculine
Sng	Singular
Pl	Plural
p1	First person
p2	Second person
p3	Third person
Present	Present tense
Past	Past tense
qst	Question

V. Conclusion

In this paper, I have presented few examples of Pashto endoclitics generation and some rules for cliticization process. The generation mechanism can be situated into any existing of linguistic theories such as Lexical Functional Grammar (LFG), Head-Driven Phrase Structure Grammar (HPSG) and Combinatory Categorial grammars (CCG). The Combinatory Categorial Grammar formalism will be chosen because of clear syntax-semantics interface particularly suited to natural language generation systems. As no theoretical and computational work has been done so far in NLG for Pashto language, therefore theoretical work has been shown in this paper for cliticization and endoclitics generation of Pashto sentences. Later on OpenCCG toolkit which is an open source natural language processing library will be used for Pashto clitics generation.

References

[1] Wikipedia: "The History of Pashto Language", (30 November, 2007). Retreived From Wikipedia, the free encyclopedia, http://en.wikipedia.org/wiki/Pashto_language.

[2] Babrakzai, F. (1999). "Topics in Pashto Syntax" , Ph.D Thesis, Linguistics Department, University of Hawaii.

[3] Din, Khan (2007), " Syntax Based De- Cliticization of Pashto text for Better Machine Translation" in the proceedings of Conference on Language and Technology (CLT07) at Bara Gali campus, University of Peshawar (August 7- 11, 2007) Page no.1.

[4] Tagey, Habibullah. (1977) "The Grammar of Clitics: Evidence from Pashto and Other Languages" PhD Dissertation University of Illinois.

[5] Kopris, A Craig & Davis Anthony R. (2005) "Endoclitics in Pashto: Implications for Lexical Integrity" Presented at the Fifth Mediterranean Morphology Meeting, Sept. 15-18, 2005, Fréjus, France.

[6] Bogel, T. (2010) "Pashto Endoclitics in Parallel Architecture" in the Proceedings of LFG10 Stanford: CSLI Publications

[7] Anderson, S. (2005) "Aspects of the Theory of Clitics" Oxford University Press.

[8] Kaisee, Ellen. (1981) "Separating Phonology from Syntax: A Reanalysis of Pashto' Journel of Linguistics, Col. 17, No. 2 (Sep., 1981), pp. 197-208 Cambridge University Press. Dost, A. (2005) "A Domain-Based Approach to 2P Clitics in Pashto" in the Proceedings of the Texas Linguistics Society IX Conference

[9] Dost, A. (2005) "A Domain-Based Approach to 2P Clitics in Pashto" in the Proceedings of the Texas Linguistics Society IX Conference

[10] Roberts, T. (2000) "Clitics and Agreement" PhD Dissertation Massachusetts Institute of Technology

Malayalam Clause Boundary Identifier: Annotation and Evaluation

Sobha, Lalitha Devi
AU-KBC Research Centre
MIT Campus, Anna University
Chennai-600044
sobha@au-kbc.org

Lakshmi, S
AU-KBC Research Centre
MIT Campus, Anna University
Chennai,600044

Abstract

Clause boundary identification has a significant role in improving the performance of different practical NLP systems. In this paper we have dealt with automatically identifying various types of clausal structures in Malayalam, a Dravidian language. The clausal sentences were collected from tourism and health domain available in the Web. We discuss about the annotation schema and the inter-annotators agreement for various clauses and also the automatic identification of clause boundaries using CRFs a Machine learning approach. To smooth the errors obtained from the CRFs tagging, we have used linguistic rules. For Inter-annotators agreement we have used kappa coefficient as the agreement statistic. The evaluation gave encouraging result.

1 Introduction

Clause identification is a shallow parsing task, where the boundaries of a clause are determined. Syntactic structure information, given by the clause boundaries in a sentence helps in improving the NLP applications. Incorporation of clause boundary identification enhances the performance of various applications such as machine translation, text-to-speech, information extraction, question answering system since it gives a deeper level of syntactic information. In English, clause is defined as a word sequence which contains a subject and a predicate. This subject can be explicit or implied. In automatically identifying the clause, the boundaries of the clauses in a sentence are marked. In the present work, we give in detail the annotation and the automatic identification of clause boundary in Malayalam. We use the machine learning approach CRFs for identification of clause boundary and use linguistic rules to correct the errors obtained from the CRF engine.

Many learning approaches were used in the clause identification task. Hidden Markov Models, Memory-based Learning, Boosting are some of them. Eva Ejerhed (1988) developed a basic clause identification system, for text to speech system to find basic surface clauses in unrestricted English text, using various combinations of finitary and stochastic methods. Leffa (1998) used a rule based method where clauses can be ultimately reduced to a noun, an adjective or an adverb regardless of their length or the number of embedded clauses they may contain. After the rule based techniques, machine learning approaches and hybrid approaches where used in clause boundary identification.

Orasan (2000) used a hybrid method for clause splitting in unrestricted English texts which used a machine learning algorithm and a shallow rule-based module. Molina et al. (2001) has used a specialized HMM approach to clause identification task where clause start and end tags were detected along with embedded clause detection. The clause identification was the shared task in CoNLL-2001 (Tjong et al., 2001).Conditional random fields is used for most of the sequence labeling tasks, such as shallow parsing by Sha (2003),named entity recognition task by McCallum et al., (2003).A multilingual method for clause splitting was done by Georgiana Puscasu (2004). Here she used the information of coordination and subordination with machine learning technique. Clause spitting was done by using conditional random fields' technique by Nguyen et.al. (2007). Alegria et al. (2008) identified systems for syntactic chunking and clause identification for Basque, combining rule-based grammars with filtering-ranking perception. An approach was presented where CRF and linguistic rules were used and cascaded by an error analyzer by Vijay et al., (2008).

There have been limited efforts on clause identification for Indian languages. One such approach is in Tamil where Vijay et al. (2009) has used CRFs based approach, where the syntactic rules are used for error correction. Daraksha Parveen et al. (2011) has done clause boundary identification task for Urdu using classifiers. They have used the machine learning technique, which has linguistic rules as features, to identify the clausal boundaries first and the misclassified clause boundaries were corrected using additional linguistic rules. Aniruddha Ghosh et al. (2010) had worked for Bengali, where they have used rules for identifying the clause boundaries and CRFs to classify the clause. In Bengali, corpus used is from NLP Tool Contest: ICON 2009, they have annotated the clause information. Hindi clause boundary information is automatically tagged using the Stage 1 parser for Hindi developed by Husain et al. (2009).

The paper is arranged as follows, in the next section we discuss about the various clausal structures in Malayalam. In the third section, we have explained about the annotation of clause boundary markers and explained the inter-annotator agreement. The automatic clause boundary identification system and its evaluation are explained in fourth section and finally the conclusion and reference section is presented.

2 Clause Structures

We describe in detail about the clauses and the clausal structures in Malayalam, one of the South Dravidian language. It is a verb final language and also a free word order language. It has postpositions, the genitive precedes the head noun in the genitive phrase and the Complementizer follows the embedded clause. It is a nominative-accusative language like the other Dravidian languages. Here, due to rich inflection, the morphology of the words contributes more information than in English which is a non-inflected language. The clause boundaries are indicated by suffixes attached to the verb. We have considered the following clauses for analysis, Relative participle clause (RP), Conditional clause (CON), Infinitive clause (INF), Complementizer (COM) and Main clause (MCL). The clause is identified by the type of non-finite verb present in the sentence. Different structures in each clause are described below.

2.1 Relative Participle Clause

The relative participle clause is identified by the relative participle suffix 'a' attached to the non-finite verb in a sentence. The relative participle (RP) verb takes all tense forms. The future form is essentially restricted to certain types of written usage (Asher and Kumari, 1997).Based on the constituents that follow the relative participle verb, the relative participle clause can have the following patterns.

RP verb followed by Noun

1. *da:hajalam kontuvarunna pla:stikk*
DrinkingWater bring+present+rp plastic
kuppikal vanapAlakar thatayunnunt.
bottle+pl forestguard+pl prevent+pres+be+pres
(Forest guards are preventing plastic bottles in which drinking water is brought.)

This is the most common structures of RP clause, RP verb followed by a noun phrase, which will take all the case markers. This NP can also be preceded by a genitive noun. In the above sentence RP verb ' kontuvarunna ' (bringing) is followed by a Noun phrase ' pla:stikk kuppikal'(plastic bottles)

RP verb followed by PSP

2. *tibattil ethunna ya:thrakka:r*
Tibet+loc reach+present+RP traveller+pl
6 divasam kont kaila:sa ma:nasasarovara
6 days psp kailasa manasa sarovar
darSanam natathiya shesham athirthiyil
worship did+RP psp border+loc
thirichethi curam katakkunnu.
come-back hairpin-bend cross+pres
(Travellers who reach Tibet ,finish the worship of kailasa manasa sarovar in 6 days and then come back to the border and cross the hairpin-bends.)

RP verb can also be followed by a PSP without NP in between. PSP's such as 'shesham','muthal' etc will follow the RP verb. In above sentence RP verb 'natathiya' is followed by PSP 'shesham'.

RP verb followed by a Noun and Adv

3. *nura patayunna thirama:lakalkk pinna:le*
Foam foam+present+RP wave+pl+dat behind
kuññunnal otum.
children run+future.
(Children run behind the waves which is foaming.)

In this structure of RP clause, RP verb is followed by a dative noun and an adverb. In the above given sentence ' patayunna ' is the RP verb followed by dative noun thiramalakalkk and adverb ' pinna:le '.

RP verb followed by a pronoun

4. *ra:vile kulakkatavil kulikka:n ettiyavar*
morning pond bath+inf reach+RP+pron
oru bhīkarajīvi natathunna puja kant
one monster perform+RP worship see
bhayann a:lukale vilichukutti
frighten+past people call.

(In the morning those people who came to have a bath in the pond got frightened seeing one monster performing worship and they went and called others.)

The RP verb can be followed by a pronoun, similar to RP verb followed by NP. Here the pronoun can be agglutinated with the RP verb. In the above sentence ' ettiyavar ' (those who reached) is the RP verb followed by a 3 person plural epicene pronoun.

2.2 Infinitive Clause

Infinitive (INF) verb does not take tense markers and the infinitive marker is 'a:n'. The infinitive clause in the sentence is identified using the infinitive verb.

5. *a:nakkuttannale ka:na:n e:rravum kututhal*
Herds of Elephants see+INF utmost
avasaram kittunna pradesam
opportunity get+RP place
añchuna:zhikathot vanama:nu
Anchuna:zhikathot is forest
(Anchuna:zhikathot forest is the place where you get utmost opportunity to see herds of elephants.)
Here the infinitive verb is ' ka:na:n ' ' to see '.
INF+Inclusive marker

6. *ka:ppa:t gramaththilute ozhukunna*
Kappat village+through(case) flow+past+RP
korappuzhayilute bott sava:ri nataththa:num
korappuzha boat riding perform+RP+inc
ka:ylil po:kanum saukaryamunt
backwater go+RP+inc has facility
(There is facility to do boat riding and also go to the backwaters in the korappuzha river flowing through kappat village.)

Here ' nataththa:num ' and ' po:kanum ' is the 2 Infinitive verbs.

2.3 Conditional Clause

Conditional clause is identified by conditional (CON) verb. The suffixes for conditional verb are 'a:l'.
CON verbs take tense markers. It occurs in present, past and future tense.

7. *ivite ninnu 3 manikkur trekkin natathiya:l*
here from 3 hours trekking do+cond
varya:ttumottayil varaya:tukale
Varayattumotta+loc Nilgiri tahr
ka:na:m
see+future+mod

(From here if we do trekking for 3 hours (we) can see Nilgiri tahr from Varayattumotta.)

The conditional verb is "natathiya:l" with the suffix "a:l". Here the embedded clause is "ivite ninnu 3 manikkur trekkin natathiya:l" "If we do trekking for 3 hours". Main clause is "varya:ttumottayil varaya:tukale ka:na:m " "can see Nilgiri tahr from Varayattumotta".
The addition of an emphatic particle 'ee' to a conditional form also occurs to express the concept of 'only if'.

8. *nurrant tha:ntiya parvathavantiyil*
Century cross+past+RP mountain vehicle+loc
mala kayariya:le uutti ya:thra
hill climb+con+emphatic ooty trip
purnnamaku
fullfilled
(Your ooty trip will be fullfilled only if you climb the hill in the centuries old mountain train.)

Here ' kayariya:le ' is the conditional verb with the emphatic particle.
Unfulfilled conditions are marked using the suffix 'enkil'. (Asher and Kumari, 1997)

9. *i: varsśaththe rathhothsavam ka:nanamenkil*
this year+acc chariot festival see-want+cond
navambar 8 muthal 16 vareyulla divasannalil
november 8 from 16 upto day+pl+loc
kalppa:ththi sandarsichcha:l mathi.
Kalppathi visit enough
(If u want to see the radhostav this year u can visit kalpathi from November 8 to 16.)

Here ' ka:nanamenkil' is the unfulfilled conditional verb.

2.4 Complementizer Clause

'ennu' is the Complementizer (COM) marker in Malayalam, which is similar to 'that' in English. The Complementizer Clause can occur in three different positions in a sentence. It can be before, after or within the main clause.

10. *ra:man varum enn kutti paraññu*
Raman come+fut that child tell+past
(The child told that Raman might come.)

11. *kutti paraññu ra:man varum enn.*
Child tell+past raman come+fut that.
(The child told that Raman might come.)

12. *kutti raaman varum ennu parannu.*
child Raman come+fut that tell+past
(The child told that Raman might come.)

Out of the three the third form is most common in the tourism and health corpus which we had selected for annotation.

13. *ka:na:mpuzha ozhukiyirunna kanththur gramam*
kanampuzha flowing+RP ka:nathur village
pinnīt kannur enna peril ariyappettu enn oru
later Kannur name known that one
abhiprayam
opinion
(There is an opinion that Kanathur village through which kanampuzha river was flowing later came to be known as Kannur.)

"pinnīt kannur enna peril ariyappettu" is the complementizer clause in the above sentence.

3 Annotation and Inter-annotator Agreement

3.1 Corpus

The clause tagged corpus used in the CoNLL Shared task 2001, is one of the first available corpus. In that corpus, they have used "S*" to indicate clause start and "*S" for indicating clause end. The corpus was presented in column format, which has word, part-of-speech, chunk and the clause boundary tags. In this style of annotation they had only marked the start and end of the clauses and the type of clause is not mentioned. In our tagging schema we have tagged the type of clauses as well as the start and end of the clause. We selected about 6415 tourism and 385 health corpus sentences from the Web and training set consisted of 5000 sentences from both the domains. Testing of the system was done with 401 unseen sentences from the tourism corpus.

3.2 Annotation

The sentence boundaries were not given in the preprocessed data. We have identified relative participle clause, conditional clause, infinitive clause, complementizer and main clause. We have used the tags {RP} and {/RP} for RP clause start and end respectively. Similarly we have used the following tags to represent the start and end tags, {INF} and {/INF} for INF clause, {CON} and {/CON} for CON clause, {COM} and {/COM} for COM clause and {MCL} and {/MCL} for main clause.

14. *{CON} ivite ninn 3 manikkur*
here from 3 hours
trekkin nataththiya:l {/CON}
trekking do+cond
{MCL} varya:ttumottayil varaya:tukale
Varayattumotta+loc Nilgiri tahr
ka:na:m {/MCL}
see+future+mod
(From here if we do trekking for 3 hours (we) can see Nilgiri tahr from Varayattumotta.)

Above example shows how the annotation is done using our schema.

3.3 Inter- annotator Agreement

We have measured the inter-annotators agreement as there could be ambiguity in identifying the start and end of clauses. Inter-annotator agreement is the degree of agreement among annotators. It is the percentage of judgments on which the two analysts agree when coding the same data independently. There are different statistics for different types of measurement. Some are joint-probability of agreement, Cohen's kappa and the related Fleiss' kappa, inter-rater correlation, concordance correlation coefficient, Cochran's Q test, intra-class correlation and Krippendorff's Alpha. We use Cohen's kappa as the agreement statistics. The kappa coefficient is generally regarded as the statistic of choice for measuring agreement on ratings made on a nominal scale. It is relatively easy to calculate, can be applied across a wide range of study designs, and has an extensive history of use. The kappa statistic k is a better measure of inter-annotator agreement which takes into account the effect of chance agreement (Ng et al., 1999).

$$k = (p_o - p_c)/(1 - p_c)$$

where p_o is agreement rate between two human annotators and p_c is chance agreement between two annotators. The results of kappa-like agreement measurements are interpreted in six categories as follows (Yalçınkaya et al., 2010).

Kappa Score	Agreement
<0	Less than chance agreement
0.0–0.2	Slight agreement
0.2– 0.4	Fair agreement

0.4–0.6	Moderate agreement
0.6–0.8	Substantial agreement
>0.8	Almost perfect agreement

We calculated the kappa score for each clause start and end and are presented in the following table.

Clauses	Start	End
RP	0.89	0.82
CON	1	1
COMP	0.63	0.63
INF	1	1
MCL	0.84	0.89

Table 1. Kappa Score

As the clause end is actually identified during the clause boundary identification task the level of agreement between the annotators should be more for clause end. But when we see the RP clause the clause end agreement is low compared to clause start. The complementizer clause is having only substantial agreement. The overall kappa score is 0.87 that means it is almost perfect agreement between the annotators.

4 Automatic Clause Boundary Identifier

We have used a hybrid method for identification of the clause boundaries, a machine learning method CRFs for the detection of the boundaries of the clause and the type of clause and linguistic rule based approach to correct the error made by the CRFs approach. The input sentences are preprocessed for sentence splitting, tokenizing, morphological analysis, part-of-speech tagging (POS) and chunking. The features are obtained from the linguistics analysis of the various types of clauses which are discussed in detail in section 4.2.The error analysis uses syntactic rules specific to certain constructions where there are difficulty in identifying the start or end by the ML method. In the following sections we give in detail both the approaches.

4.1 Conditional Random Fields (CRF)

CRFs are an undirected graphical model. Here conditional probabilities of the output are maximized for given input sequence (Lafferty, 2001). This technique is used for various tasks in NLP.

Learning: Given a sample set X containing features $\{X_1,........, Xn\}$ along with the set of values for hidden labels Y i.e. clause boundaries $\{Y_1,..........,Y_n\}$, learn the best possible potential functions.

Inference: For a given word there is some new observable x, find the most likely clause boundary y* for x, i.e. compute (exactly or approximately):

$y^*=\text{argmax}_y P(y|x)$

Linear-chain CRFs thus define the conditional probability of a state sequence given as

$$P_\Lambda(\mathrm{s}|\mathrm{o}) = \frac{1}{Z_\mathrm{o}} \exp\left(\sum_{t=1}^{T}\sum_{k=1}^{K} \lambda_k f_k(s_{t-1}, s_t, \mathrm{o}, t)\right),$$

where Z_o a normalization factor over all state sequences, fk (s_{t-1},s_t,o,t) – is an arbitrary feature function over its arguments, and λ_k (ranging from $-\infty$ to ∞) is a learned weight for each feature function. A feature function may, for example, be defined to have value 0 in most cases, and have value 1 if and only if s_{t-1} is state #1 (which may have label OTHER), and s_t is state #2 (which may have START or END label),and the observation at position t in o is a relative pronoun or a conditional marker. Higher λ weights make their corresponding FSM transitions more likely, so the weight λ_k in the above example should be positive since the word appearing is any clause marker (such as conditional or relative clause marker) and it is likely to be the starting of a clause boundary. Here we have used CRF++ tool which is available on the web (Kudo, 2005).

4.2 Features

The performance of the machine leaning technique depends on the features used in learning. The features used in our approach are word, pos, chunk, morph information and the clause type information. The type of clause is determined by the suffix the non-finite verb takes and this is used as one of the features. The chunk boundaries are more important as a feature since most of the start and end boundaries of the clause matches with that of the chunk boundaries. Part-of-speech information provides the context and definition of the words in a sentence.

Consider example 1

da:hajalam kontuvarunna pla:stikk
DrinkingWater bring+present+rp plastic
kuppikal vanapAlakar thatayunnunt.
bottle+pl forestguard+pl prevent+pres+be+pres
(Forest guards are preventing plastic bottles in which drinking water is brought.)

In the above clause tagged sentence the word "kontuvarunna" is the RP verb and its POS is VM and chunk information is B-VGNF and morph information is v+rp. These information is used by the ML approach to learn the patterns.

4.3 Error Analyzer

The error analyzer module is used for detecting the erroneous clause boundary markings done by CRFs module. For example consider the below given sentence.

15. *athinu sesśam athuvare uuzham kaththu*
after that till then opportunity wait
nilkkunna komarannalum janannalum onnichch
stand+RP komaram+pl and people+pl together
a:vesalahariyote dikkukal muzhannunna
excitement in all directions echoing+RP
tharaththil marankampu kont ksśethraththinre oot
kind wooden stick with temple bell-metal
meñña melkkurayil atichchu kont munnu
thatched+RP upper roof beating psp three
pravasyam valamvekkunnu
times rounds
(After that those komarams and people waiting for an opportunity together in excitement, rounds the temple 3 times while beating the bell-metal thatched upper roof with a wooden stick in an echoing sound .)

From the output generated for the above sentence it was noticed that RP clause ending was not marked at *"athinu sesśam athuvare uuzham kaththu nilkkunna komarannalum"* and RP start was not marked at *"janannalum onnichch a:vesalahariyote dikkukal muzhannunna tharaththil"*. For detecting the errors, the training data (gold standard data) itself is given as test data to CRFs system. The erroneous clause boundary marked sentences which are filtered out by the error analyzer module are further analysed using linguistic rules. The error patterns derived by processing the gold standard data are compared with the output of the CRFs module to detect the incorrect clause boundaries marked by the CRFs module.

4.4 Grammatical Rules

The rules are used to treat the erroneous clause boundary markings done in the CRFs module. The rules are used to identify the unidentified clause boundaries in the given sentences. It actually fine tunes the CRFs output. The grammatical rules used in the clause boundary identification work are as follows.

To get the relative participle clause boundary

If the current token is a PSP, the previous is a RP verb then current PSP is the probable RP clause end.

-1 VM+RP
0 PSP=1 RP clause end

If the current token is NP and the previous one was a relative participle verb and if the next token is not a PSP then the current token becomes the RP clause end.

-1 VM+RP
0 NP RP clause end

To get the conditional clause boundary

If the current verb has a conditional marking suffix, then the current verb is marked for probable conditional clause end.

0 VM+CON = 1 CON clause end

To get the infinitive clause boundary

If the current verb has the infinitive suffix then the current verb is marked for probable infinitive clause end.

0 VM+INF=1 INF clause end

To get the complementizer clause boundary end

If the current word is a complementizer "ennu ", the previous word is a finite verb followed by a noun phrase. The COM clause end boundary is marked.

-1 VGF
0 Complementizer=1 COM clause end
1 NP

Once these rules are run, the probable clause start positions are marked based on the probable clause ends marked.

For the example 14 when Boolean entries which obey the linguistic rules was given as a column in training data the output was free of errors.

4.5 Evaluation and Discussion

There were 358 relative participle clauses, 36 conditional clauses, 7 complementizer clauses and 264 main clauses in the testing sentences. We measured the performance in terms of precision and recall and F-measure, where precision is the number of correctly recognized clauses to the number of clauses marked in the output, recall is the number of correctly recognized clauses to the number of clauses and F-measure is the weighted harmonic mean of precision and recall.

Clauses	Recall	Precision	F-measure
RP open	96.65	89.87	93.14
RP close	69.51	73.1	71.3
CON open	54.3	100	70.4
CON close	80.6	100	89.26
MCL open	58.46	52.77	55.47
MCL close	90.9	89.22	90.05
INF open	33.33	40	36.36
INF close	66.67	80	72.73
COM open	57	100	72.6
COM close	100	100	100

Table 2. Performance of the system

On analyzing the performance tables, it is clear that the propagation of errors from the prior modules affect the performance, as this identification tasks requires all the three analysis, morph analysis, POS and chunk information to be correct, to introduce the tag at the correct chunk. Consider example below

16. thotine kavachchuvaykkunna
Stream+acc straddle+pres+RP
cheriya palam katann valaththott thiriññ
small bridge go right turn
kayariya:l irumpunnikkara vare nattu vazhi
Ascend+cond irumpoonnikkara till land

(If you turn right and ascend through the small bridge straddling through the stream there is land till irumpunnikkara.)

Here there is an RP clause followed by a conditional and main clause. But the output of the system tags RP clause properly, but the Conditional clause start is not marked properly.

17. *annu rajkumari paraññа kathhakal*
That day princess tell+past+RP stories
kett pamp pirrenn thirichchupoyennan aithihyam
listen snake next day went back history
(The history is that the snake went back after hearing the story told by the princess.)

In such type of sentence formation the RP clause end was not properly marked.

5 Conclusion

In this paper, we have discussed about some clausal structures in Malayalam, described about annotation of clause boundaries in Malayalam sentences. Finally we have explained about the automatic clause boundary identifier using CRFs. We have discussed about the factors affecting the identification task. The system can be further improved with more rules.

References

A. and Uria, L. 2008. Chunk and clause identification for Basque by filtering and ranking with perceptrons. *In Proceedings of SEPLN.*

Aniruddha Ghosh, Amitava Das and Sivaji Bandyopadhyay. 2010. Clause Identification and Classification in Bengali. In *Proceedings of the 1st Workshop on South and Southeast Asian Natural Language Processing (WSSANLP, 23rd International Conference on Computational Linguistics (COLING)*, Beijing, 17-25.

A. McCallum and Wei Li. 2003. Early Results for Named Entity Recognition with Conditional Random Fields, Feature Induction and Web Enhanced Lexicons. In *Proceedings of CoNLL-2003*, Edmonton Canada, pp. 188–191.

Antonio. Molina and Ferran. Pla. 2001. Clause Detection using HMM. In *Proceedings of CoNLL-2001*, Toulouse, France.

Constantin Orasan. 2000. A hybrid method for clause splitting. In *Proceedings of ACIDCA 2000 Corpora Processing*, Monastir, Tunisia, pp. 129 – 134.

D. Parveen, A. Ansari, and R.Sanyal. 2011.Clause Boundary Identification using Clause Markers and Classifier in Urdu Language,*12th International Conference on Intelligent Text Processing and Computational Linguistics CICLing.*

Eva Ejerhed. 1988. Finding Clauses in Unrestricted Text by Finitary and Stochastic Methods.In *Proceedings of the 2nd Conference on Applied Natural Language Processing*, Austin Texas, pp. 219-227.

Erik F. Tjong Kim Sang and Herv`e D`ejean. 2001. Introduction to the CoNLL-2001 shared task: clause identification. In *Proceedings of the 2001 workshop on Computational Natural Language Learning.* Toulouse, France.

Fei Sha and Fernando Pereira. 2003. Shallow parsing with conditional random fields. In *Proceedings of HLT-NAACL03.* pp. 213–220.

Georgiana Puscasu. 2004. A Multilingual Method for Clause Splitting. In *proceedings of the 7th Annual Colloquium for the UK Special Interest Group for Computational Linguistics.* Birmingham, UK. pp. 199-206.

H.T. Ng, C.Y., Lim, S.K., Foo. 1999. A Case Study on Inter-Annotator Agreement for Word Sense Disambiguation. In *Proceedings of the {ACL} {SIGLEX} Workshop on Standardizing Lexical Resources {(SIGLEX99)}.* Maryland. pp. 9-13.

Husain,S.,Gadde,P.,Ambati,B., Sharma, D.M.,Sangal, R. 2009. A modular cascaded approach to complete parsing. In *proceedings of COLIPS International Conference on Asian Language.*

R.E. Asher, and T.C. Kumari. 1996. *MalayalamRoutledge*, London and New York.

Sobha.L, and B.N., Patnaik. 2002. VASISTH-An Anaphora Resolution System for Malayalam and Hindi. *Symposium on Translation Support Systems,* IIT Kanpur.

Taku Kudo. 2005. CRF++, an open source toolkit for CRF. http://crfpp.sourceforge.net .

Vilson J. Leffa.1998. Clause processing in complex sentences. In *Proceedings of the First International Conference on Language Resource and Evaluation.* Vol 1, pp. 937 – 943.

Vijay Sundar Ram, R and Sobha, Lalitha Devi. 2008 Clause Boundary Identification Using Conditional Random Fields. In *Lecture Notes in Computer Science, Proceedings of the 9th international conference on Computational linguistics and intelligent text processing Springer.* Verlag. pp. 140-150.

Vijay Sundar Ram,R T. Bakiyavathi and Sobha. L.2009. Tamil Clause Identifier. *PIMT Journal of Research.* Patiala. Vol.2. No.1, pp. 42-46.

Vinh Van Nguyen Minh Le Nguyen and Akira Shimazu. 2007. Using Conditional Random Fields for Clause Splitting. In *Proceedings of the Pacific Association for Computational Linguistics.* University of Melbourne Australia.

Author Index